Your Business Growth Playbook

Breakthrough Strategies to Scale Your Business for
Business Owners Who've Outgrown Hustle

Jeremy B. Shapiro

Asandia Press

Early Endorsements

"Growing your business is hard. Yet leveraging the practical, tactical advice found in *Your Business Growth Playbook* can make it a whole lot easier. Shapiro equips entrepreneurs with actionable strategies, derived from real-world examples and the shared insights of diverse business owners, to not only boost revenue but significantly improve profitability. By warning about common pitfalls and providing appropriate remedies, this playbook is your guide to breaking free from stagnation and achieving lasting, profitable growth and impact."
- Matt Abrahams, Stanford Graduate School of Business Lecturer

"*Your Business Growth Playbook* delivers the concrete strategies essential to scaling and achieving sustainable profitability for any entrepreneur looking to move beyond mere hustle. Shapiro brilliantly cuts through the theoretical fluff, providing a framework for amplifying profit. His robust range of customer acquisition models aligns perfectly with the real-world, disruptive approaches I have used as a serial entrepreneur, 4x exit founder, and growth strategist. This is THE direct, implementable playbook for founders determined to overcome plateaus and get back to scaling."
- Phil Masiello, MBA, 800razors.com Founder, 4x Exit Founder

"*Your Business Growth Playbook* is exactly that. A playbook for smart business owners that helps them avoid the hustle while achieving greater results. Jeremy is helping entrepreneurs step out of struggle and into scale!"
- Alex Sanfilippo, Founder, PodMatch

"I've known Jeremy for a long time and have truly admired his direct and impactful communications style. It reveals Jeremy to be highly skilled deeply thoughtful innovator and someone you want by your side in business. I've been waiting (impatiently) for him to create this fantastic resource. In it, you'll find truly timeless sound and principled business advice that deliver breakthrough business growth strategies and tactics that work. I am making it part of the required reading list for all the companies in my portfolio. Devour it. Mark it up. Dog ear the pages. And then buy another."

- Stephan Little, Managing Partner, Zero Limits Ventures

"Hustle only gets you so far - with anything difficult. It doesn't matter whether it's a crazy physical feat or building a company that's worked with 100,000 merchants, you need solid strategy and the right approach to pursue your goals. *Your Business Growth Playbook* cuts through the fluff and shows you tactical levers for real, sustainable profit. It's a no-BS roadmap for entrepreneurs who know that growth comes from strategy, not just effort."

- Brad Weimert, Easy Pay Direct | Beyond A Million

"*Your Business Growth Playbook* is full of concrete, realistic, actionable tips with just the right blend of 'I can do that right now!' and 'Not sure if I'm ready for it, but I'll try.' Definitely worth a read no matter what industry you're in."

- Megan Preston Meyer, Entropy Cottage Publishing

"I'm a small business owner advising other business owners on their company value, and following Jeremy's framework and strategies in *Your Business Growth Playbook* will not only increase the value of your business, it'll make it more satisfying to run."

- Ben Towne, CPA/ABV/CFF, Principal, Towne Advisory

"Jeremy Shapiro has created the ultimate playbook for business owners who've outgrown hustle but haven't yet unlocked their full potential. His simple formula cuts through the noise to show you exactly what levers to pull for maximum growth."
- **George Sudarkoff, Award-Winning Executive Coach**

"Having gone from quitting my job through my first business collapsing to then building a 7 figure business – and then doing it again! – I can say that *Your Business Growth Playbook* clicked with me at a deep level. Jeremy Shapiro nails what actually drives growth beyond just hustling harder as a business owner. His core framework in the book showed me exactly where to focus for consistent growth. Plus, it rightly puts profitability front and center, not just chasing gross sales, and dives deep into understanding and maximizing customer value – insights that are gold."
- **Vandita Joshi, Serial 7 Figure Business Founder and CEO, Faro**

"*Your Business Growth Playbook* is a must-read for business owners who've hit a ceiling and are ready to break through it with clarity and confidence. Shapiro cuts through the noise of generic business advice with real-world strategies, grounded in his own entrepreneurial experience and decades working with other business owners. The book doesn't just inspire—it equips you with a practical, flexible framework to grow revenue and profit without burning out. Whether you're feeling stuck, scaling, or simply seeking smarter ways to grow, this playbook delivers the tools, mindset, and momentum to take your business to the next level."
- **Peter Mu, CFP® ChFC®, Founder and CEO, Wealth Cairn, LLC**

"After decades of helping entrepreneurs turn overwhelmed operations into profitable, freedom-focused businesses, I can confidently say: *Your Business Growth Playbook* is a must-read for any small business owner ready for a real breakthrough—or a growing business looking to scale without burning out. Jeremy Shapiro cuts through the noise with a refreshingly

clear framework built around three core growth levers. He shows how even modest improvements in just one area can unlock significant jumps in both revenue and—critically—profitability. Jeremy equips readers with actionable, real-world tools to make smarter decisions, avoid costly detours, and build momentum that lasts. Whether you're stuck at a plateau or planning your next big leap, *Your Business Growth Playbook* is a resource I recommend without hesitation to the business owners I advise."
- Dr. David Hilton, DBA, MBA, M.Ed., Business Strategist / Coach

"In a world where 'hustle' often overshadows 'heart,' Jeremy Shapiro's *Your Business Growth Playbook* stands out. I found Jeremy's subtle encouragement to think about the broader impact of your business beyond just the financials particularly compelling. As a lifelong entrepreneur and mentor to entrepreneurs, I believe this playbook offers a clear path to build a legacy of meaningful impact, achieving freedom not just in time or choice, but profoundly in purpose."
- Sheila Farragher-Gemma, Strategic Partnerships Consultant

"As someone who's audited over 25,000 businesses and helped achieve over \$1 billion in savings, I've seen countless entrepreneurs chase revenue while their profits evaporate. Shapiro's *Your Business Growth Playbook* tackles the real challenge: converting revenue into sustainable profit and freedom. What sets this book apart is Shapiro's unflinching focus on the fundamentals most business owners ignore. He offers a clear growth formula that maximizes both revenue and profit margins. This work isn't theory – it's a practical playbook for building wealth, not just income. Every serious business owner needs this book."
- Marc Freedman, Chief Cost Advisor & Founder, Expense To Profit

"This book should be on the bookshelf of every entrepreneur. Filled with clear, specific, and actionable processes for growing any type of business, Shapiro also loads the book with terrific illustrative stories, basic equations that make business math easy to understand (even for mathphobes), and evergreen advice about how to identify problems, develop solutions, and implement systems to grow your business in comfortable, sustainable, and ethical ways. A must-read for any entrepreneur who wants to run a business like a real CEO."

- Michele Rosenthal, CH, PCC, MNLP. My Trauma Coach

"Small business owners, I know what you're thinking: Not another business growth playbook! But believe me when I say, this is the last business growth playbook you will need. While most books promising business growth give you a cookie cutter framework that probably won't work exactly the way you hope (since your small business is anything but cookie cutter), Shapiro's book gives you the tools you need to create your own playbook. I really love how this book gives you simple, easy-to-understand formulas that can be applied to give you a plan for growth that you can implement. Shapiro makes business growth feel doable, not overwhelming."

- Emily Crookston, The Pocket PhD

"I was deep in the trenches of scaling my demolition business, and like a lot of business owners, I had hit that growth ceiling where more hustle wasn't the answer. The wisdom Jeremy shared helped me build smarter systems, focus on profit, and ultimately scale the business to the point where I was able to exit successfully. Reading *Your Business Growth Playbook* feels like sitting down with Jeremy again, no fluff, just sharp, real world strategies that work. I especially appreciated how he reframes plateaus as something to expect and plan for, not fear. That mindset alone is powerful. This is the kind of book I wish I had in my hands years ago. Whether you're stuck, scaling, or prepping for a big leap, this book is pure gold. If you're serious about building a business that's both profitable and sustainable, Jeremy's playbook delivers. Five stars, without hesitation."

- Ryan Crownholm, Founder, MySitePlan and DirtMatch

Edited by Hugh Barker
Cover design by Caerus Kourt
Author photos by David Friedlander

Library of Congress Control Number: 2025920075

ISBN: 979-8-9985866-0-6 ebook, 979-8-9985866-1-3 paperback, 979-8-9985866-2-0 hardcover

For information about special discounts available for bulk purchases, conference attendees, and educational needs, contact Asandia Press at bulkorders@asandia.com

Visit the book's website at YourBusinessGrowthPlaybook.com

First edition 2025

Published by Asandia Press
440 N. Barranca Ave #2330
Covina, CA, 91723 USA

To my wife, Emily, for always encouraging me with love, lending a listening ear, asking great questions, and saying yes to so many adventures.

Contents

1. Introduction

"The secret of getting ahead is getting started. The secret of getting started is breaking your complex overwhelming tasks into small manageable tasks, and then starting on the first one."
- Mark Twain

No matter the size of your business, you're going to hit some plateaus as you grow.

Plateauing means the growth has stalled, business has stagnated, and new customers are harder to find. Plateaus make you feel stuck, like no matter how much more - or harder - you work, you're not able to stave off a shrinking business or get back to growing your revenue.

Expenses keep getting higher but revenue isn't keeping up. The next cancellation or slow month could edge you closer to being out of business. More hustle just isn't working anymore.

Even the often idealized "up and to the right" "hockey stick" growth curve plateaus once you zoom out.

And in the great game of business, it's not about avoiding these plateaus; it's about expecting them, anticipating them, and planning for them before you hit them.

What got you to where you are today isn't working as well. Maintaining the same pace of growth becomes ever more challenging as you need to pivot, innovate, and expand.

So *how* do companies just like yours course correct?

What are the tactical and strategic methods that they choose to find new growth and get "unstuck"?

How are businesses like yours implementing the *right* strategies to increase not just revenue but also profits?

Those are exactly the questions we're going to be answering in *Your Business Growth Playbook* with real world examples that you can implement in your business today.

You'll be developing your playbook as you go and choosing which strategies you want to use. And before you plateau again... I invite you to return back to this guide to choose the next strategy you want to use. Again. And again.

The growth strategies we'll be covering in the bulk of this playbook fall into one of three categories we'll be sharing that make up a simple formula you can use to quickly understand - and improve - your gross revenue.

We'll dive deep into this formula in Your Three BIG Levers to Scale Revenue, but for now there are two important things to know about this simple - yet powerful - formula.

First, improving just ONE of the variables in our simple calculation will help to increase top line revenue for your business.

Second, improving the *right* variables can even help you to improve the *profitability* in your business.

Fear not the mention of "formulas" and "variables", though. The variables are few and the formulas - while powerful - are easy to understand and use in your business. We'll be speaking to both our logical left brains with the math and tactical strategies and also to our story-loving right brains that remember how we *feel* from stories.

For example, in Filling Your Top of Funnel, we'll go into how a brick and mortar retail store owner came into our Mastermind Group and - like many business owners - was feeling that plateau in her business.

Even though she was seeing success, and was profitable, her growth had plateaued. She was stuck. In the room, however, she learned about a growth strategy that she didn't even know existed – an "unknown unknown" – from another member in our group. She was then able to implement this newly learned tactic over the course of the next month between our meetings.

This simple change added an entirely new sales channel to her business increasing her overall revenue *and* profitability.

And at long last, just like the member she learned the growth strategy from, she was able to literally click a button and see new sales come in: something she had never been able to do before that day.

And from the other side of the table, in Increasing the Quantity of Customers, we'll cover how that very same e-commerce store owner unlocked a whole new stream of business by leveraging a best practice shared by the brick and mortar retail store owner!

And (spoiler alert!) many of these strategies come from what I call the "cross pollination" of ideas between diverse business owners. These are the real gems that us entrepreneurs typically only share behind closed doors. And now, we're flinging those doors wide open, so you can share in these same polished gems, too.

For example, we'll look at how a traditional medical practice grew revenues in non-traditional ways while creating happier and more loyal patients...

We'll even show how an education business ran a few simple experiments that helped to *double* revenues at the time of purchase.

And for our ambitious readers with dreams of creating the next "deca-corn", we'll pull real world examples from some of the biggest brands out there and how they grew revenues using the same exact simple formula that you can use in your business today.

These are the strategies that I've successfully used for over 25 years in my own businesses as a serial entrepreneur, with coaching and consulting clients in their businesses, and with members of our Mastermind groups.

From my first real business that I launched while still in my teens, building out my first team and client portfolio, to the businesses that gave me the freedom to live abroad, with cashflow coming in literally while I slept, to the businesses that highlighted me on the morning radio, front page of the newspaper, and evening TV news, entrepreneurship has been at the center of who I am as a person, a husband, a dad, an athlete, and a community member.

Entrepreneurship has afforded me the freedom of time, and the freedom of choice. Entrepreneurship is what has opened so many doors for me in life and enabled me to live a life my younger self didn't even know was possible.

My experience comes not just from my own businesses but through my work with individual entrepreneurs. This includes everything from one-on-one work to small group masterminds to workshops with hundreds of people to stages in front of thousands of business owners. This depth of experience has allowed me to "connect the dots" on the patterns that get results in business.

Whether advising clients or implementing for clients, it always comes down to this playbook of strategies I've spent my career refining.

These strategies are practical, tried, and true.

Like you, I'm both a visionary and an implementer. That is, I'm the typical entrepreneur with endless ideas as well as the pragmatic executor of ideas. It drives me nuts as a reader when a book wants to talk *about* an idea but not actually share *how* to get it done.

That being said, if you are an "oooh shiny" entrepreneur who has trouble getting stuff done, I hope this book will be more than just an inspiration for you. I hope it will help you to identify opportunities and create a plan. But there's no way around saying this: it will be up to you to actually execute your plan. Only action drives change.

You have to actually create the plan and then execute it. You can do this on your own, hand it over to your implementer to get done in your business, or hire in help to execute and implement.

Either way, action will always get better results than great ideas that never see the light of day.

None of the stories or strategies shared in the chapters ahead were mere ideas. They've all been implemented, which... is how you get results.

At a conference years ago, in a room full of entrepreneurs like you and me, I heard a great perspective on the difference between ideas and implementation from our event host and keynote presenter, Dan.

Dan said *"If we sat you in the corner with all of your ideas and came back to check on you a year from now, all we'd find is you still sitting there, just the same, only covered in cobwebs."*

Action gets results.

The story of the Wagoner and Hercules illustrates this well.

In the story, a wagoner is driving his cart along a muddy road when he gets stuck - literally in a rut. After praying to Hercules, the god of strength, for help, Hercules appears and tells the wagoner to put his shoulder to the wheel and push.

The wagoner does so, and with Hercules' help, he is able to free his cart. Hercules then tells the wagoner that he will always be there to help him, but only if the wagoner helps himself first.

The story of the Wagoner and Hercules is a reminder that we all have the strength to overcome our challenges, but we must be willing to actually *implement* the ideas that we're given. And if you're worried about feeling overwhelmed - as so many business owners are - in Prioritization and in Your Action Plan, we'll go over how to pick what to do first and where to focus your energy and resources.

Each of our individual challenges is unique to us.

Some challenges were created by our own actions, and many by circumstances outside of our control.

Either way, we can't just sit in a rut and hope and pray that things will be different.

Like the wagoner, my one ask of you is that, when you're feeling stuck in your business or in a rut, you don't just *read* this book.

Commit to actually *implementing* the strategies that I will be sharing.

To help you with implementation, after each strategy in this playbook, you'll find a ***Put it into Action!*** box to help you move from idea to implementation.

Even if you only implement *one* of the strategies from my formula, that can make an incremental difference. And sometimes... that's all the momentum we need to get unstuck and truly grow.

2. The Biggest Obstacle to Growth and Profit

"Growth is never by mere chance; it is the result of forces working together."
- James Cash (J.C.) Penney

Often, when we're looking to grow our business, we find ourselves in a catch 22.

"If I had more revenue, I could afford to market and grow my business."

Remember what happened with WeWork, and its billions of dollars of loss?

It was set up as a company that provides shared workspaces, and its revenues grew rapidly in the 2010s. However, the company was also *losing* money, and its losses grew even faster than its revenues. In 2019, WeWork's losses were over $1 billion that year - on revenues of $1.8 billion.

There were several reasons for WeWork's losses. One reason was that the company was spending heavily on growth, such as new office locations and marketing. Another reason was that WeWork's prices were often *below* its costs, which meant that the company was *losing* money on each new member.

WeWork's financial problems came to a head in 2019 when the company's initial public offering (IPO) was canceled. This caused WeWork's valuation to plummet, and the company was forced to lay off thousands of employees.

In 2020, WeWork filed for bankruptcy. The company emerged from bankruptcy in 2021, but it was still not *profitable*. WeWork's story is a cautionary tale about the dangers of growing top line revenue without looking at *profitability*.

This is why revenue isn't always what matters for our growth. *Profitability* is what really makes a difference.

How else can growing revenues get you into hot water?

Consider a sales-team-based business like a local car dealership that focuses on unit sales at the expense of profit. Their volume-focused salespeople may offer discounts and deals to sell a car, losing money on each one. They'll hit their "number of vehicles sold" target, while still losing money on each sale.

You can't make up for a lack of profit with volume!

When you focus your business on gross sales at the expense of profit, you'll find yourself in all kinds of trouble.

This is why chasing gross sales without considering profitability can result in *unsustainable* growth. You're burning cash reserves - or credit – in order to grow.

Your business may appear to be growing rapidly, but without a focus on profit, you may not be able to cover its expenses, which leads to financial instability.

You're forced to keep pouring money into the leaky bucket you're calling a business to make up for the losses. The money you're flushing away may be your own hard earned cash or borrowed from investors, lenders, or the banks - all who will want it back.

Prioritizing gross sales instead of profit can also lead to short-term expenses over longer term investments. In our chapter on Prioritization we'll get into organizing priorities and decision frameworks that can help make heads and tails of the four categories of "priorities", but for now, let's focus on what can grow your *profit*.

A sure fire way to stay "stuck" in your business is to spend your day in firefighting mode of dealing with the *today* vs. the right longer term investments for *tomorrow*.

Without a focus on what will generate profit, your business may not have the cashflow or financial resources to invest in innovation, research and development, and team growth. That is where all of your innovation comes in to expand into new markets, launch new products, and more.

We'll cover just this kind of innovation and launching of new products more in depth in our chapter Expanding Your Product Portfolio as this is essential for long-term growth and success.

Lastly, one way that companies often increase gross sales is by discounting their products to increase volume in the short term.

However, beware of this approach. Discounting your products may feel like a growth strategy, but it is more disastrous than you might imagine! You could be losing 75% or more of your profit through even a small discount, as we'll see below.

In fact, discounting goes against one of our key strategies, which we cover in our chapter on Increasing your Prices.

Discount promotions may sound attractive, but they're probably gutting your business – and you might not even know it.

We see promotions all the time where companies discount their products and services, but those businesses never share what that actually means financially *behind* the scenes – and why it leads many businesses to lay off staff or close up shop entirely.

Promotions can begin a business' death spiral, delay consumer purchases, and put you out of business before you even realize it.

As an example, say you have $4mm in Gross Revenue for the year.

And your Cost of Goods Sold ("CoGS", i.e. what those sales cost you) is $1mm (25%).

Your Gross Profit is $4mm – $1mm = $3mm, or 75%.

Let's say your business expenses are $2.5mm (62.5%).

That leaves you with a Net Profit of $500k (12.5%). Not bad.

Now... let's say you decide you want to increase gross sales by offering a 10% discount...

You now have $3.6mm in Gross Revenue ($4mm - $400k)

Your CoGS is the same at $1mm (25% -> 27.7%)

But... your Gross Profit takes a hit (75% -> 72.2%)

And since your expenses are also the same at $2.5mm, they have grown as a proportion of Gross Revenue... (62.5% -> 69.4%)

This brings your Net Profit down from $500k to $100k! (12.5% -> 2.7%)

You just lost 75% of your profit.

Scarily, that's barely profitable!

Using the same example numbers above, let's try a 15% off promotion:

$3.4mm in Gross Revenue

-$1mm CoGS (same)

-$2.5mm in Expenses (same)

= -$100k (NEGATIVE One Hundred Thousand) in Gross Profit

THIS is how many businesses start their death spiral out of business.

You CANNOT discount your way to profitability!

Our chapter on Decreasing the Amount of Each Transaction dives deeper into this - and how these kinds of holiday promotions ended up almost bankrupting one business, leading to a downgrade in its credit rating and mass layoffs.

We are also going to cover what happens psychologically to your customers when you get into the habit of running discount promotions - and how other businesses have gone the opposite direction – building customer loyalty based on other factors besides price.

So... if discounting your products to increase your gross sales is a bad idea, how do we increase both gross sales *and* profitability?

That's exactly what we're going to cover in the rest of this book.

You see, acquiring customers costs money. And the more margin you have *up front* the more you can spend to acquire customers. Our Chapter on Increasing the Quantity of Customersis all about acquiring new customers, but before we get there, there is a foundational idea that – once understood – will allow you to outspend your competition even if you *do* lose money up front.

This all comes down to Customer Lifetime Value (CLV), next up after we establish a quick baseline for where you're at... which is what our next chapter is all about.

3. Baseline Self Assessment

"The first step toward getting somewhere is to decide you're not going to stay where you are."
- J. P.Morgan

You're successful. You know your products. You know how to sell what you've got to your ideal customer. But you're also ready to scale beyond that.

After arriving in Wonderland, Alice was told by the Cheshire Cat *"If you don't know where you are going, any road will get you there."*

The same advice applies to us in business - and life in general.

So, before we dive into the playbook, let's figure out where you are. Then we can make a plan to get you where you want to go.

To do this, let's get a baseline assessment and identify where in your journey you are.

These are easy yes/no questions that you should answer based on where you are now - not where you want to be or what you aspire to grow to. Be honest.

Bear in mind that not every single one of these questions will garner a Yes and not all of these will apply to you or your business – and *that's okay*.

Nobody gets a 100% on this, even the most perfect established business.

By the time you finish this book, *many* of your Nos may become Yesses. And *some* of your Yesses will get even better.

You can complete this online, too, at YourBusinessGrowthPlaybook.com under Resources.

Simply check, underline, or circle the ones that are true.

- I know my Customer Lifetime Value (CLV)

- I know my Customer Acquisition Cost (CAC)

- I know my CAC and CLV by lead source

- I know the levers in my business that I can easily move to increase revenue

- I know each of the steps in my sales funnels

- I actively track each step in my funnels

- I know how effective each conversion is between the steps in my funnel

- I regularly review my funnel stats and any changes in conversions

- I have a continuity program in place that generates recurring revenue from my customers

- I regularly add new products and services to my offerings

- I regularly launch my new offerings both internally and externally

- I have multiple tiers of product/service offerings

- None of my funnel steps are converting above 90%

- I offer third party affiliate offers that I believe in to my list

- I use bounceback offers to bring customers back to purchase again

- I have a loyalty program to reward my customers

- I have consumables that customers buy from me as they use them or run out

- I have various packages / formulations for my products

- I regularly update, refresh, and relaunch my products

- I run customer appreciation events

- I know my churn numbers for my continuity programs

- I regularly track churn and any changes in churn

- I know how to reduce my churn and actively manage it

- I have upsells and add-ons available during purchase

- I increase my pricing regularly

- I have niche versions of my products and services

- I have bundles for my products and services

- I actively cross-sell "across the aisle"

- I offer payment plans

- I offer third party financing

- I offer tiered bonuses / gifts with purchase

- I offer customization and personalization for a fee

- I offer volume discounts for quantity purchases

- I allow my customers to prepay for their continuity programs for a discount

- I offer downsells

- I know who my top vendors are that I pay the most money to

- I've worked my way up my supply chain to launch new businesses

- I know how to fill the top of my funnel with new prospects

- I actively and successfully use direct mail

- I actively and successfully generate business from SEO

- I actively and successfully use content marketing in my business

- I actively and successfully use PPC to generate new business

- I have an active affiliate partner program that generates regular new business

- I successfully use cold outbound email to generate new business

- I successfully use cold calling to close new business

- I actively use Social Media to generate new business

- I have a successful PR campaign and process in place with regular media appearances

- I use traditional advertising in my business to generate new revenue

- I actively get referrals from past customers, existing customers, and my network

- I actively repurpose my products and services for new niches

- I know where my funnel is "leaky"

- I know how to fix the leaks in my funnel

- I know my largest expenses categories

- I speak to my biggest vendors at least annually to discuss expense reduction

How do you feel about your Yesses and Nos from the assessment above?

Already getting some good ideas and inspiration?

Good!

Now that you know where you are today, you're ready to get started on making a better tomorrow.

The rest of this book is dedicated to helping you move as many of those Nos to Yesses and... and to taking the areas that are already a Yes and doing *even better*.

With that, let's jump into one of our most foundational topics that will

provide us with the first two of the three key variables we need to understand our finances and the rest of the tactics in our playbook...

4. Understanding Customer Lifetime Value (CLV)

"The success of your business depends on your ability to create lifetime customers."
- Shep Hyken, Author, The Loyal Customer

In the short term, business owners often look at getting "the next sale" or just "getting more customers" without considering what a customer is *really* worth longer term.

Every one of your customers has a *lifetime* value.

It's not the same across all of your customers, but the value exists for each of them. And if you know what you're doing, you can even *forecast* how much a customer is going to spend with you in the future.

For example, if you have a restaurant, bringing a customer *back* to dine with you again increases their Customer Lifetime Value (CLV).

Or, let's take a look at business mastermind King Gillette. And, yes, King was his actual name, not a nickname!

King made an absolute fortune from his business model, breaking down the initial sale into multiple parts and deconstructing the idea that a consumer only buys a good product once.

Gillette, founder of the Gillette company, is often credited with coming up with this idea. The story goes that he got frustrated with his dull straight razor and realized there was a market for a razor with cheap, replaceable blades.

The razor + razor blade model is a clever business model that involves selling a product for super cheap, or even at a loss, to get customers hooked on buying related products later on. The strategy builds a huge base of loyal customers who keep coming back for more.

Over time, this "razor blade model" has evolved to include any business that offers a cheap or free product that requires customers to make repeated purchases of another product.

Think of how cable companies used to give away Digital Video Recorders (DVRs) or cable boxes but then charge monthly fees to use them. Or how Peleton sells you an exercise bike one time that's mostly useless without its content subscription.

But you don't have to give away products to use this model.

Companies like Sony and Microsoft initially sold their video game consoles at a loss. They made up for it later by selling gaming subscriptions, software licenses, and other add-ons.

This strategy allowed them to leverage the razor blade model and rake in profits from their dedicated and committed customer base.

Or take Keurig, the coffee pod company. They sell their automatic coffee makers at a low price, but make all their real long term profit on the sale of their coffee pods.

Then there is Apple. Not only do they sell their iPhones at a high price, they make almost pure profit on all App Store sales, and then also of course on the sale of software, accessories, and services.

All of these businesses understand the value in increasing the *lifetime* value of a customer beyond a single transaction.

So how do you *calculate* your Customer Lifetime Value?

Simple. We look at the transactions that a customer makes.

Specifically, we consider how many times they transact with you over their lifetime ("Frequency") and how much they spend on each transaction ("Amount").

CLV = Frequency x Amount

So, let's say that you have a continuity business where a customer sub-scribes to your membership program or your publication.

Perhaps customers stay with you on average for 18 months. And they pay $100/month.

Your CLV is 18 x $100 = $1,800

Now, let's say we make a few changes and you're able to keep your cus-tomers with you 2 months longer, on average.

Your CLV is now 20 x $100 = $2,000

Now, let's suppose we increase your prices to $120/month.

Your CLV is now 20 x $120 = $2,400

As you increase your customer lifetime value this way, you've not only increased your gross sales, but also, if it is done right, increased your profitability.

Increase this and you may not even need more customers!

The founder Alex Turnbull tells a great story about this with his bootstrapped business.

He was chatting with another CEO who was balking at his $5mm ARR (Annual Recurring Revenue) business with only 5 employees.

She had 120 employees and a fresh round of $30mm in funding.

Of the two companies, can you guess which one was *actually* profitable?

The other CEO asked him how he scaled his business and he simply answered *"We don't. We're profitable."*

The best part of this was that in his "small business" - generating five million in revenue a year - 47% of that was *pure profit*.

That kind of profitability buys you quite a lot of freedom. This might include the freedom to work on products that your customers actually want instead of chasing new customers or discounting your way into new business.

Consider Costco Wholesale, a membership based discount warehouse club for grocery and home good products.

Costco has a membership retention rate of over 92% meaning that in a given year, over 92% of their customers keep their membership.

Even better, if we look at their gross revenue, while membership fees make up only 2% of their revenue, 73% of Costco's gross profit comes from its membership fees. This means that while membership is an almost insignificant part of their gross revenue, it accounts for almost all of their profit.

Or how about financial/wealth advisors or life insurance brokers?

They often make a percentage of their total assets under management - regardless of the markets being up or down - or on policies that renew.

So long as their customers don't change advisors, cancel their life insurance policies, or die... advisors make a fee every single quarter (or year) from their client base. To say the least, in our model above, their Frequency is *high*.

Financial advisors retain over 94% of their clients, on average, year to year, according to McKinsey. Even if you're a terrible advisor, in the lowest 10th percentile, you can still expect to keep 84% or your clients year over year.

If you're pretty good at your job, in the 90th percentile, history shows that you'll *retain 98%* of your clients!

Again, that Frequency number is *high*. And that means higher CLV.

So, what can you do when you have a high CLV?

For starters, a higher CLV lets you outspend the competition to acquire new customers.

In finance parlance, we're referring to your Customer Acquisition Cost or CAC.

You may also see this referred to in the Pay Per Click (PPC) world as CPA or Cost Per Acquisition.

In one of my earlier subscription-based businesses, when I was first learning about CLV, I had a question that nobody seemed to be able to answer for me.

My question was how to calculate Customer Lifetime Value when you still have active customers who haven't reached the end of the time with you yet.

In my business, for example, we had plenty of subscribers who'd been with us since the beginning, so we didn't know the upper end of what our CLV would be.

This meant that, when we acquired a new customer, since we couldn't know the maximum or average lifespan, we didn't know how to forecast their future CLV.

Especially with a newer subscription or SaaS business that has most early customers still enrolled, it seemed that calculating CLV would be impossible.

It wasn't until years later when I had my first real Software as a Service (SaaS) business that I learned the answer I'd been looking for. I was fortunate to have the opportunity to nerd out behind the curtains of larger more established SaaS businesses and deep dive into the numbers with the CFOs. It was then that I learned about what is now the industry standard math for figuring this out.

It all came down to a variable we haven't talked about yet. And that's Churn.

Churn, in your business, is how many customers you *lose* in a given time period as a percentage of how many customers you *started* that time period with.

Churn = Customers Lost in Period / Customers at Start of Period

So let's say in your newer membership site business you have 100 customers at the start of the month. Over the course of the month, you gain 20 new members, but you lose 3.

In calculating churn, we don't care about the number of new members, or your net growth, we're simply looking at what you've *lost* in that time period.

So in this example, if you started the month with 100 and lost 3, your *monthly churn* would be 3/100 or 3%.

Monthly Churn = 3 / 100 = 3% per month

If you started your year with 1,000 subscribers and by the end of the year had lost 80, your *annual churn* would be 80/1,000 or 8%.

Annual Churn = 80 / 1,000 = 8% per year

Regardless of how many new customers you get in that time period, some of whom may stay with you for years and have only paid you a fraction of their future CLV, you now know roughly how many will *leave* in a given time period.

Again, we don't care how many customers you gain in that period for churn. So if you have a big new launch and gain 1,000 new customers doubling the number of subscribers you have, that doesn't help the fact that you lost 80 of the customers you started with.

Now that you know about Churn, you can figure out how long a customer is going to stay with you.

Simply divide 1 by churn.

Customer Lifetime = 1 / Churn

So if your churn was 3% per month, as in the example above, you know customers will stay with you for about 33.3 months.

Monthly Lifetime = 1 / 3% = 1 / 0.03 = 33.3 months

Or, with our annual churn example above of 8%, we divide 1 by 8% to get 12.5 years.

Annual Lifetime = 1 / 8% = 1 / 0.08 = 12.5 years

Now that we know our Churn - or our Lifetime - let's plug it into the formula to figure out our CLV.

For the same period as you're using for your Churn calculation, get your Frequency and Amount and multiply by Lifetime - or more simply just divide by Churn.

CLV = Frequency x Amount x Lifetime

CLV = Frequency x Amount x (1 / Churn)

CLV = Frequency x Amount / Churn

Let's say that in a given year, you started with 1,000 customers who each transacted on average 10 times with you at an average order value of $97 and over the year you lost 150 of those customers.

For that year, your:

Frequency is 10

Amount is $97

Churn is 15% (150 / 1,000 = 0.15)

Lifetime is 6.67 years (1 / 0.15 = 6.67)

So your CLV is 10 x $97 / 15% = $970/0.15 = $6,467

CLV = (10 x $97) / 15% = $6,467

Even though you're only looking at one year's worth of data, you're able to use your Frequency, Amount, and Churn to calculate your *potential* CLV, even for brand new customers.

Now, over time, and depending on lead source, Customer Profile, and other variables, your churn may vary. This isn't a number you calculate once and never look back at.

In fact, you'll probably want to dashboard this number and track your churn rate trends over time.

What impacts your churn?

You might have brought on a cohort of new customers that weren't your ideal customer, so they churn sooner. Or perhaps you targeted your advertising better, and attracted much higher quality members who stick with you longer.

That's okay. You want to see your churn and your trends. That will then let us improve our churn, which we'll cover in our chapter on Strategies for Reducing Churn.

And now that you know what churn is, you know that decreasing churn means your customers stay with you longer, which increases their Frequency of Transactions, which... increases their CLV!

And that brings us to our next chapter - and the focus of most of our book: we're going to look at the three big levers in your business that can scale your revenue - and profits.

5. Your Three BIG Levers to Scale Revenue

"The journey of a thousand miles begins with one step."
- Lao Tzu

Imagine if you had a lever you could pull to increase the revenue – and profit – in your business...

What if you had THREE levers you could pull that all got the same result?

Well, good news... Hold onto your hats. You DO have these levers!

In every business – yes, even yours – there are three major "levers" you have to increase your revenue and profits. Together these three variables – F, A, and Q – make the formula that I call your "FAQs to More Profit".

Adjusting any one of these levers can increase revenue in your business.

We've already touched on two of these (F = Frequency and A = Amount) in our previous chapter on Customer Lifetime Value, but the third – Q – is probably where you've spent most of your energy over the years while trying to scale your business.

However, before we get into the third variable, and how to improve each of the three variables in my "FAQs to More Profit" formula, let's look at what Gross Sales and Profit really are in a business.

In any business you have an important number to look at – it makes up half the equation for profit.

First we have to figure out what your Gross Sales are. This is a number that your accountant or bookkeeper will have handy for you in your financial reports, or that you can look at when reviewing your Total Sales. You can even just look at the deposits going into your business bank account.

Gross Sales or "Income" is simply the total amount of money that you take in as a business from all of your sales. This is before deducting any of your Cost of Goods Sold (COGS), your commissions, your returns and refunds, your expenses, and so on.

Now, is Gross Sales how much money you're really making?

No. It's just what you sold in total.

For certain businesses, margins are razor thin, so on $5mm in revenue, there might only be $100k in actual profit.

That's why, after we figure out our Gross Sales, we will then need to figure out what our profit is.

There are a few schools of thought on calculating the profit in your business - especially your small business - but the overall theme is that you subtract all of your expenses during the same time period and you end up with the profit of the business.

This is what you commonly look at on your Profit and Loss (P&L) report.

This can vary; in very small businesses, typically under $200k in annual gross sales, what you as the business owner take out will usually be a significant portion of the gross revenue. In a larger business, this will be a much smaller percentage.

So given your two numbers here – you simply subtract Expenses from Gross Sales (Income) to get Profit.

Profit = Income - Expense

So if you want to increase your profits, you either... increase your income, or reduce your expenses.

While this playbook is mainly about increasing the income part of the equation, we do touch on expenses too, in our chapter on Expense Reduction.

The first big lever to increase revenue and profit in your business we introduced in the previous chapter on Customer Lifetime Value is **F** for **Frequency of Transactions**, meaning how often a customer buys from you.

The second lever is again **A** for **Amount of Each Transaction**, meaning how much a customer spends each time they buy from you.

And the last is **Q** for **Quantity of Customers**, meaning how many unique customers buy from you.

Your business' sales volume is simply Frequency of Transactions x Amount of Each Transaction x Quantity of Customers or more simply:

Gross Sales (Income) = F x A x Q

For example, in a business, if a customer, on average, buys from you 4 times over their lifetime (F=4), the average sale amount is $250 (A=250), and you attract 1,000 customers (Q=1,000), then Gross Sales = 4 x 250 x 1,000 = $1,000,000.

If you have a subscription business, your average customer sticks with you for 18 months at $500/mo, and you have 200 customers, your Frequency (F) is 18, your Amount (A) is $500, and your Quantity (Q) is 200. Gross Sales is then 18 x 500 x 200 = $1,800,000.

What do these numbers look like in your business? Fill in the blanks below to find out.

_____ = _____ x _____ x _____

Gross Sales = Frequency x Amount x Quantity

Good. Now you have a baseline for where you are now.

What difference will some small changes make, though?

That's what we'll explore in our next chapter on Revenue Multipliers Through Leverage.

6. Revenue Multipliers through Leverage

"Success is the result of small efforts, repeated day in and day out."
- Robert Collier

Now you might think that making a small improvement in each area would be *additive*; that would mean that, if you increase each area by 10% that you'd see an overall 30% improvement.

But that math would be wrong.

See, when we're dealing with percentage improvements, it's not additive... it's *multiplicative*.

A small 10% increase in each of F, A, and Q leads to a 33% increase in sales – not a 30%.

A 20% increase in each F, A, and Q, leads to a 73% increase in sales – not 60%!

These multipliers increase *each other* – not just the base.

That's what we call "Leverage"!

Just how powerful is leverage?

Let's take a look at the British Cycling team under the leadership of Sir Dave Brailsford.

In 2003, he began implementing a strategy called "marginal gains," which essentially focused on making 1% improvements in every area that could possibly influence how well the team could ride.

Dave and the British Cycling team got to work making marginal improvements to things like tire grip, seat comfort, and aerodynamics. They went as far as using special hand-washing techniques to reduce the chances of riders catching a cold. They even tested pillows and mattresses to see which provided the best night's sleep!

What effect do you think all these small improvements had?

Well, having won only a single Olympic gold medal since 1908, the British Cycling team was transformed from mediocre to great; they dominated the 2008 Beijing Olympics, winning 60% of the available gold medals.

Then, in 2012, they set seven world records and nine Olympic records at the London Olympics.

The British Cycling team remains one of the best in the world today, simply by focusing on these incremental small improvements.

It's like what Warren Buffet - and many others – have referred to as the "8th Wonder of the World"... That is, Compound Interest.

Compound interest describes the growth of an investment over time when the interest earned each year is added to the principal and earns interest in subsequent years.

This "compounding" effect is a powerful force that significantly increases the value of an investment over time, even with relatively modest interest rates.

What makes compound interest so powerful is... time.

The longer an investment is allowed to grow, the more time the interest has to compound and add to the principal. Even a small difference in the investment period can result in a significant difference in the final value of the investment.

But the most important factor that contributes to the power of compound interest is *reinvestment*.

When interest is earned, it is added to the principal and then earns interest in subsequent years. This means that the interest earned in early years is *compounded* over many years, leading to a snowball effect.

This "snowball effect" is exactly what's at play when we make small improvements in our business to F, A, and Q.

It's the same "marginal gains" that made the difference for the British Cycling team.

Implementing a few simple strategies – which we will get into in the next chapter – will allow you to get this snowball effect, too.

Adjust these levers, charge a premium, i.e. charge more than your competition, keep your customers with you longer, and get more customers just like them at little to no cost.

Next, it's time to get into our playbook of tactics, the first being increasing the Frequency of Transactions!

Increasing the Frequency
of Transactions

"Repeat customers can be the lifeblood of any business, turning one-time purchases into a reliable revenue stream."
- PayPal

It costs a lot of money to acquire a customer. And hopefully you know exactly how much it costs you to get a new customer (Hint: This is the Customer Acquisition Cost or CAC, which we mentioned earlier in our chapter on Understanding CLV).

However, once you have a relationship with your customer, it costs much less to keep them. This is where you want to then increase the Frequency of transactions.

There are many ways that you can have your customers buying more frequently from you; in this chapter we're going to lay out some of the top tactical strategies you can use to do just that.

Subscriptions / Membership / Continuity

You have a tremendous amount of value to offer your customers, more than you could ever deliver in one upfront purchase. A continuity subscription provides recurring revenue to you in your business *and* provides long term value to your customer.

That last part is key: your continuity program, in whatever form it is, has to actually provide *value* or you either won't get enrollment, or you'll have higher churn.

Think about Amazon's Subscribe and Save program, where they deliver additional *value* to you by auto-shipping you what you need and saving you money at the same time.

Or look at the difference between a car wash selling you a one-time wash vs. a monthly package auto-billed to your card. You just show up and get your car washed when you need, often in an express line, without having to pay.

Or consider a large one-time software purchase that quickly gets old vs. an indefinite monthly fee to have the latest version of the software.

Or how about selling a property and "cashing out" one time as compared to keeping it and renting it out long term for cash flow?

Are you getting the idea behind continuity and how it provides *value* to the buyer now? Good! Now we'll dig into what makes these programs successful.

In 2007, Amazon tried out a new idea as they launched their now famous Subscribe and Save program. The idea was pretty simple - let customers sign up for regular deliveries of all kinds of products, from household essentials to personal care items, and give them a discount of 5-15% off the regular price.

This made it easy for customers to never run out of the things they used most, and save money in the process.

The program was developed by the product and engineering teams at Amazon as a way to not only boost customer loyalty but *also* to increase recurring revenue.

If they could get people hooked on regularly scheduled deliveries, Amazon could better predict demand *and* optimize their whole supply chain and logistics operation.

While Amazon doesn't share specific numbers, analysts estimate the Subscribe and Save program is bringing in *billions* in annual revenue and is a major contributor to the company's retail and logistics profits. It's become a key part of their strategy to build up a huge base of loyal, high-value customers who rely on Amazon for their regular household needs.

The program has helped Amazon cement their position as the go-to online shopping destination for tons of households - not just for one off purchases but for automatic shipments. And it's given them a reliable and *predictable* stream of recurring revenue to keep fueling their massive growth.

Yes, discounting is a danger as we cover in Decreasing the Amount of Each Transaction, but - and here's the important caveat - Amazon doesn't use this consumer discount to get a sale with less profit. With Subscribe and Save, the customer pays less to increase the Frequency of Transactions and

Amazon *also* reduces their supply chain costs. Everyone wins.

Software as a Service (SaaS)

Going even further back for another great example of this strategy, let's look at the software industry.

Businesses had always been used to making one-time purchases for software and then upgrading when they needed, which often meant contract negotiations, purchase orders, and sales teams. Entire IT teams would then be responsible for installing, licensing, maintaining, and managing the purchased software.

Then, in 1999, Marc Benioff launched Salesforce.com, with a very different approach to software. Instead of selling the license one time and then again having to sell to the same customer later on, why not instead put the software online and bill customers for access to the service on an ongoing basis?

That was the beginning of the entire Software as a Service (SaaS) business model, a model we all take for granted today. Their radical idea was evident in their slogan, "The End of Software," which took on a entrenched and established industry directly.

Beyond SaaS being a better model for the actual customer in so many ways, it made for much more predictable *recurring* revenue for Salesforce.

These days, with so many "no code" solutions, you don't even need to hire developers to add an SaaS platform to your product line. It's easier than ever to create a solution that you can use both for lead generation (increasing Quantity of Customers) and for your existing customer base (increasing Frequency of Transactions).

Businesses today typically have *dozens* of SaaS subscriptions to run their operations. Just look at your credit card statements or financials and you'll see all those SaaS subscriptions!

Larger businesses may even have *hundreds* of SaaS subscriptions. Both the buyer (the customer/business) and the seller (the software maker) can budget and count on those recurring transactions.

Membership Sites and Courses

Membership sites, courses, and programs are another great recurring revenue add-on for your business that can increase the number of transactions a customer has with you.

A common strategy that I've used with clients that were experts and authors is to help them deliver more content ongoing to their customers through a continuity program or membership program. While an online course is also wonderful, it's dated the moment you publish it.

A membership program enables your members to not only stay up to date on the latest members only content that you create, it can give them access to a community of other members, too!

Creating a membership site is as easy as adding a membership site plugin to your existing website, or simply creating a new website using one of the many platforms out there.

For an up-to-date list of the platforms we like, check our list at under Resources at YourBusinessGrowthPlaybook.com

Then, you not only preload some initial content for new members, but also continue to add new content going forward for your members. These can be training videos, new course modules, industry updates, and more.

A doctor we were working with used this exact strategy to add an entirely new revenue stream to his business.

Previously, he had a traditional cash-based brick and mortar private medical practice. Patients came in when they needed medical care, paid for it out of pocket, and only returned again in the future when they needed more care.

By adding on a wellness membership program, he was able to share the latest in the world of medicine and wellness with his patient base, answer their live questions, and provide priority care for his members.

And... he added a new stream of revenue to the business, and created an even more loyal customer base, both of which in turn ALSO dramatically increased the Frequency of Transactions.

Newsletters, Continuity, and App Subscriptions

This is the exact same strategy that many businesses use when they add on a paid newsletter.

This can be an old fashioned print newsletter that is sent out to paid subscribers monthly - think one step removed from a magazine. It can be a paid digital newsletter delivered privately to members on a platform like Substack. Or it can simply be an email newsletter that you send out to your list of paid subscribers.

Wim Hof, known as "The Iceman", is a Dutch extreme athlete and motivational speaker famous for his ability to withstand extreme cold temperatures. He has developed a method involving cold exposure, breathing techniques, and meditation, which he claims provide various health benefits like reduction in inflammation, improved recovery after exercise, and enhanced metabolic rate.

After setting multiple Guinness World Records for feats like longest time in direct contact with ice and running a half marathon barefoot in the Arctic, and participating in scientific studies exploring the physiological effects of his methods, he began traveling the world giving talks and workshops promoting his "Wim Hof Method" as a way for people to better withstand physical and mental challenges through training and self-discipline.

This is the classic path of an expert turned teacher turned author and speaker.

But what else did he add onto his product line, that you can emulate?

He launched a simple - and free - mobile app. You can use it for breathwork sessions, training, and more. But there's also a paid version of the app that gets you even more premium features.

This simple addition of a mobile app provides more value to his customer base - *and* adds a new recurring revenue stream to his business.

And these days, like with the web based SaaS platforms in the previous section, it's become easier than ever to launch a mobile app platform like Wim. Mobile apps - like web apps - can be launched with "no code" drag and drop app builders. Unless you're getting very specialized or sophisticated, you don't even need a developer!

For an up-to-date list of tools we like for "no code" apps and websites, go to the Resources section of YourBusinessGrowthPlaybook.com

Any of these continuity models work - from SaaS to membership sites to newsletters. They all come down to customers paying you on a recurring basis for ongoing value.

And if you're still unsure about adding in a subscription component to your business, consider the fact that three quarters of direct to consumer brands have a subscription-based offering, with the subscription economy (globally) projected to be USD $1.5 *trillion* USD in 2025.

Put it into Action!

- What kind of continuity program could you add into your business to start generating recurring revenue?

- Could it be an auto-ship program for recurring product purchases? How about a paid print, online, or email newsletter?

- Alternatively, might it be a membership site and/or membership community? Ongoing group coaching or members' calls? A SaaS platform or paid app?

A recurring revenue product is just the first of the many ways that we can increase that Frequency of Transactions.

In the next section we'll dive into a ton of additional proven strategies you can use to increase the Frequency as well.

Expanding Your Product Portfolio

So you have at least one core product or service in your business that your customers have purchased from you.

This means your customers all have a number of things in common. They are a certain type of buyer with similar challenges and aspirations.

Perhaps they are in the same industry. Or even the same geographical market. Or the same age demographic?

What else do customers like yours need?

One favorite strategy to have customers buy from you again is to create something else to offer that they need. This is typically product or service that complements what you already offer.

Walking distance from my home is a wonderful brasserie that's open for dinner and late night for fancy drinks. Other than that, they're closed during the day.

Recently, the restaurant was purchased and the new owners opened a complimentary restaurant - using the exact same space - to offer breakfast, brunch, and lunch.

They leveraged the same real estate, the same local customer base, the same kitchen, the same staff, and so much more to greatly expand what they can offer.

This was effectively a new product being offered to the same market. Brilliant.

One of my clients was running an ecommerce business selling physical products to a very niche market. The way he fast tracked his growth to a seven-figure business in almost no time was through continual product launches serving the same market.

A part of his team was even dedicated to researching and formulating new products, sourcing ingredients, putting together the sales copy and marketing, and then lining up the recurring product launches with each new release.

There was literally a spreadsheet and a calendar lined up for upcoming product launches.

Often, when a new product was pre-launched to existing customers, it sold out before it even made it onto the website for the general public to purchase. (See more on this under Loyalty Programs)

All of those sales were increasing the frequency of transactions with existing customers. That was before the product ever had a chance to attract *new* customers!

This simple strategy allows your existing customers to buy from you again. And it has the add-on effect of allowing you to attract more customers into the Top of Your Funnel (ToFu), which we'll cover in our chapter on Increasing the Quantity of Customers.

Consider a trip to the amusement park or museum with the family.

Not only do you pay for your entrance tickets, but then you also pay for your parking, snacks, lunch, photos, and pass upgrades. These are all additional offerings that the same vendor added on to offer you value.

As much as 50-75% of the revenue an amusement park generates is from sales *after* the admission ticket! A full 30 to 40% of total amusement park revenue actually comes from food and beverage sales, followed by 10-20% from retail merchandise, and so on.

No matter how niche your business or target market is, you'd be surprised at how many subgroups exist within your prospect and customer base.

It's like zooming into a fractal, as you go deeper into your customer avatar. Within each group are sub groups, and within those, the same is true again. Remember the 80/20 rule, where you focus entirely on the 20% of your work that gets you 80% of the result? As soon as you do that, you'll see an 80/20 split *within* that 20%. Rinse. Repeat.

As you create offers to serve the niches *within* your customer base, you'll find yourself not only with a broader product portfolio, but also serving prospects who never bought from you before.

This amazing phenomenon is always a surprise to the business owners I work with. One of the most memorable times this came up was working with a business primarily selling data to individual investors for a monthly membership of $19/month.

Many prospects were interested in the results they could get from the membership - investing smarter - but... they never bought a membership for the data.

And it wasn't because of the cost. Not at all. It's because the membership would have required them to *use* the data and do more work to get the results they wanted.

It'd be like selling auto-ship groceries to busy professionals too busy to cook their own meals. The subscription was valuable, but *not to the type of customer that wasn't going to use it.*

We decided to experiment with a much higher cost offer that would be entirely "done for them", where they didn't have to do the work to get the result. Instead of putting in *time*, they could put in *money*.

Suddenly, in addition to existing customers buying at a now much higher level, prospects from the list who had *never bought over the years* were showing interest. And then buying. At many tens of thousands of dollars each.

All because a new product was added to the portfolio. That new product served the same *broader* audience, but a different niche *within* the audience: buyers who wanted the same result, except they had more money and less time.

This is like a gym having their machines and free weights section, classes, and personal training. All of their members have the same broader goal of health, wellness, and fitness. Some want to do it on their own with the machines and weights. Some want an instructor and class to work out with. And others want one-on-one personal training. These are all niches within the same customer base.

Compare that to a gym that doesn't have classes or personal training. They serve the same *broader* audience, but aren't serving two of the higher end niches within that audience.

One last example for you: We all need to eat, and even in the niche of people who want home cooked meals, there are varying levels of service providers serving different niches within the niche. Consider professional chef-prepared meals made for you in your kitchen as opposed to auto-shipped groceries. Both are valuable services serving the same *broader* audience, but the niches within the audience value different products and services.

This strategy of adding in additional products to your portfolio not only

increases the Frequency of Transactions by selling a new thing to existing buyers, but also the Quantity of Customers by converting existing
prospects on the list into first time high end buyers.

Put it into Action!

- What do your ideal customers all have in common?

- What common challenges do they face? What keeps them up
  at night?

- How else can you serve them with an additional product or
  service?

Additional Product / Service Tiers

Beyond adding *different* products and services, another great way to reduce churn, keep your customers with you longer, and continue increasing that frequency of transitions, is to split out your product or service *tiers*.

If you have one level of service, look at how you can add on higher levels for your customers that grow or need more, or how you can add on lower levels, to keep your customers that no longer need your current tier.

You've probably seen membership programs that have a Silver, Gold, and Platinum, or Basic and Premium, or some sort of differentiation between tiers.

This lets customers - and ideally members - ascend or descend as needed, but still stay with you.

The Financial Times (FT) was a traditional print newspaper that made an interesting transition as they added in two new service tiers beyond their print subscription.

For decades, the FT was the go-to publication for the global business and finance crowd, known for its salmon-pink paper since its inception in 1888. (A side note on marketing, they chose this paper color so that they would stand out on the news stand next to the typical white and gray pages of other publications at the time.)

But then the internet came along and shook up the whole media landscape...

FT saw the writing on the wall and knew they had to adapt.

In the early 2000s, they started pouring a ton of resources into building their digital presence - launching a slick website, mobile apps... the whole nine yards. The goal was to reach a younger, more tech-savvy audience and capitalize on the growing demand for news and information online.

But transitioning from a print-first model to a digital-first one wasn't easy. FT had to figure out how to balance their print and digital offerings in a way that worked for both their existing readers and this new wave of online consumers.

At first, they tried the "print-first" approach, treating the digital version and digital only content as more of a supplement. But as more and more people started getting their news online, the FT realized they needed to flip that script and put digital front and center.

So in the late 2000s, they started experimenting with different subscription tiers and landed on a brilliant three tier model.

They offered a print only subscription, a digital only subscription, and a subscription to *both* at a higher price point.

The problem was that subscribers weren't seeing the value of adding on the digital, if they were already a print subscriber, so nobody was taking them up on the digital subscription.

What they did was adjust the tiers so that you could subscribe to digital only for one low price, the print for a higher price, or - as a promo - you could get both for the print price.

Suddenly subscribers who had been choosing digital instead of print jumped *up* a subscription tier to a higher price plan and started getting print *and* digital.

Fast forward, and nowadays, FT has over a million subscribers, and has retained many of them because of their digital subscription option and the "value add" of having access to their content online in addition to the print subscription they were used to.

This model works for more than just subscriptions, it also applies to one-off purchases.

Look at Disney. They charge admission to their parks, which every attendee has paid for in one way or another.

Some of those ticket holders, however, upgrade to a higher tier to get to the front of the lines on their favorite rides more easily. This is an additional transaction on top of their entrance.

There's an even higher tier, however, that serves an even more upscale audience. For thousands of dollars, you and your family can have a VIP guide take you around the park for much (but not all) of the day. They get you into any ride you want when you want. They get you reserved tables at restaurants when you like. And they are your personal concierge for the whole day.

All three of these tiers allow you to enjoy a day at the park - they just offer different tiers of service and value to three different avatars.

Like most of the strategies that improve the Frequency of Transactions, this *also* expands their market.

See, some customers were already paying for a premium Disney experience before the VIP program was rolled out. But they weren't coming back because of long lines. It wasn't until the VIP experience was offered did they begin to come back again - just now at a higher level.

On the other end of the spectrum, many Disney park visitors were finding the increasing pricing hard to stomach and could no longer afford to return.

Disney offered lower pricing on their slower days to attract visitors who couldn't afford to visit on their regular ticket price days. This kept the park full, and brought back customers who were more price sensitive.

This fourth tier was still getting buyers access to the park, and was still effectively the same product, just at a *lower* service tier.

What about if you offer expert services? How can you expand that?

A common strategy that I like to use with experts who are used to being paid high fees per hour or project and are looking to leverage their time more is to expand their product offering (see above) to also offer a course on how to get the result they offer consultatively.

This is effectively the downsell for customers who can't afford them just yet but *also* lets folks try and accomplish a task on their own before then seeing the value in having the work done *for* them by the expert.

This increases that Frequency of Transactions beautifully.

A prospective buyer can now start at the lowest tier - a book or course - and then work their way up through additional transactions to what was previously the only service offered.

This strategy commonly splits out your service offerings to three tiers that your customers can ascend:

1. I'll show you how to do it

2. I do it with you

3. I do it for you

Most businesses like yours start with just one of those tiers - which is a great place to start.

Your job is to extend those service tiers.

Put it into Action!

- What additional product, subscription, or service tiers could you add into your business?

- How can you help customers afford to do business with you at a lower cost tier or get a more premium experience at a higher tier?

- Do you have offers addressing customers looking to learn vs. be coached vs. have it done for them?

Expanding Your Funnel from the Inside

All too often, I encounter founders who have big funnel plans for their new business - especially for online businesses.

They've seen the deep funnels of other businesses and map out their "tripwire" or "free plus shipping" or "lead magnet" offer and then add in a half dozen upsells and downsells and future tiers and set about creating all the sales pages for each step of their funnel.

And that's all before they even know if the start of their funnel will work or if their market has any interest in what they're building!

I always advise to start with a Minimum Viable Product (MVP) first to see if you're resonating with your target audience and getting some traction.

Only after you're able to start getting some sales do you then go and expand your funnel by adding in additional steps.

The additional tiers covered in our previous tactic can certainly be a great starting point, but let's assume you already have two products in your ascension ladder.

What we typically do next - especially if there's a big jump in pricing between two of your steps – is to insert a product or service tier *between* your existing steps.

Over time, a mature business may even have a dozen different service levels that customers ascend through over time as they grow.

Let's take a high end paid consultant, for example.

One of our clients was paid hourly and by the project for the consulting work that he offered. As his calendar was booking up with more appointments, he kept on raising his prices, and bringing on more staff to backfill and support him.

When he found us, we helped him to scale from 1:1 work to 1:many by adding in a live training course. That additional funnel step allowed folks to learn his best practices through a course, and then use in their own business.

By adding in that earlier step, three important things happened:

1. Prospects who would never have been able to hire him at his high fees could now transact with him and become first-time customers.

2. Prospects who were looking to do it themselves could now transact with him and become first-time customers - instead of hiring a consultant

3. Prospects who were considering hiring him could now get to know him and learn how to do what they really should - and afterwards likely would - be paying him to do.

All of the outcomes led to getting MORE customers (increasing the Q), more revenue, more profitability (because of teaching 1:many), and... something even better because of the higher Q.

After we added that course to the funnel, we added in another step to the middle - between the course and the high end consulting. We added in a membership program (see the start of this chapter on Subscriptions / Membership / Continuity!), so when these first time customers purchase his course, many of them also then enrolled in his membership program. This then increased the Frequency of Transactions for his customers, too!

And after we had the course and membership program online - in addition to the boutique consulting - we added in a higher-end live event.

Over time, we established the event model, then we added in a high-end group coaching option for event attendees.

Step by step we inserted more options between the lowest end sale and the highest end sale.

But this was *only* after proving out each step of the funnel and getting enough volume through the funnel.

The goal isn't to craft and build an entire funnel before launch. That runs contrary to the MVP model.

The goal is instead to launch as soon as possible, so you can start delivering value, proving a product market fit, and generating revenue.

Only *then*, with volume and a proven funnel step, do you add additional steps into the middle of your funnel as you scale.

Put it into Action!

- Do you already have multiple offers that customers typically buy sequentially in your funnel?

- What additional offers can you insert between your existing lowest end and highest end offerings?

- Where is the biggest price jump between your existing offers and what might go between those steps?

Affiliate Offers

Your customers need more than you have to offer alone. Other products and services exist in the market that you don't need to create, but that your customers want or need to buy.

The good news is that many companies will happily pay you a referral fee (or affiliate commission) to sell their products to your audience.

Recommending products that you believe in and/or use yourself to your customer base lets them continue to transact with you - either directly or indirectly.

In the world of affiliate offers, the most common strategy is for you to simply offer an affiliates' product to your list and the purchase is made directly with your affiliate partner. Your affiliate partner then pays you a commission of the sale.

The other way of doing this is that your customers buys the affiliate offer from you directly, your affiliate partner then fulfills the order, and then you pay your affiliate partner.

Affiliate offers aren't just limited to online purchases. Affiliate offers can also be made in person, like at a live training event or conference.

If you've ever been to a live event where some of the speakers have a product or program of theirs to sell, and everyone goes to the back of the room to purchase... it's the event host who is typically processing the full amount of the sale and then paying the speaker their portion of the sale.

And remember, these additional purchases are on top of what attendees have paid to be at the event!

It's not unusual at a paid live event for attendees to make 1-3 additional purchases from the invited guest speakers with something to sell.

You may even find that you have what are called Hyper Buyers at your events who will buy everything you and your guest speakers have to offer!

This affiliate offer strategy can be such a money maker that there are even entire businesses that generate revenue *solely* through affiliate offers to their list. Their goal is to continue to grow their list so that they can send out affiliate offers.

That's right: they have *zero* products, *no* inventory, and *no* support team.

More commonly, though, businesses like yours will *add* revenue by running occasional affiliate offers to their list, not build their entire business on *just* affiliate offers.

Without list growth, however, at some point, you'll start to see diminishing returns on solely running affiliate offers to your same list.

For this strategy to work in the longer term, you need to not just continue to grow your list, but continue to deliver value to your list along the way.

So where do you find affiliate offers to share with your list?

One option is the various affiliate marketplaces where companies list their affiliate programs and you can sign up for them online.

But the easiest approach?

Look at where you're already spending money. The products and services that you already use, love, and recommend anyway, likely have an affiliate program or partner program.

If you don't see it promoted on their website, just search online for the company name and the phrase "affiliate program." If you still can't find it, reach out to your vendor and ask.

Once you're signed up, you'll get tracking links and ideally some "swipe" content, like text and images that you can use to promote that business. Then it's just a matter of sharing this content to your list.

This can be done passively just on your website, within content or articles, where it naturally makes sense.

This can be done digitally and more actively in outbound email promotions or social media posts.

This can be done even more actively in person, like in store, or from the stage at your events.

One important note, your local/federal laws likely require you to disclose when you're compensated through affiliate links or offers. Check up to make sure that you're doing whatever you're supposed to be doing from a disclosure standpoint.

Put it into Action!

- What affiliate offers could you run to your list?

- Which of your vendors do you love and would highly recommend to your list?

- What third party products would serve your customer list?

Bounceback Offers

Once a customer does business with you, what can you do *during* that transaction to bring them back again?

In the restaurant industry, these are called "Bounceback" offers and the whole point of this marketing strategy is to encourage customers to make a repeat purchase. They are typically offered in the form of a discount, convenience, or other incentive, and are usually valid only for a limited time period.

An effective bounceback offer can help you to not only increase customer loyalty, but also drive repeat purchases (increasing that Frequency!), generate additional revenue, and improve customer satisfaction.

You've probably been on the receiving end of these before. Let's say you're dining at a restaurant. You've finished your meal, and the waitstaff bring you your check. Along with the check - or even printed directly on the receipt - is a bounceback offer to encourage you to return.

Typically you'll get this offer *after* you've finished your meal and it's only valid on your next visit within a limited time period.

The offer might be for a free appetizer, a buy one get one (BOGO) offer, a discount, or anything else that would get you to come back and spend again.

Coffee and donut chain Dunkin Donuts experimented with bounceback offers and store owners found that by adding in a bounceback offer, customers, even during off-peak hours, increased 200%. It was so successful, that they rolled the program out to the rest of their stores.

You might even see these kinds of offers with a consumable good that you buy in a store or online, like a discount on your next order of dish detergent, pasta, pencils, etc.

Some sneaky sellers on Amazon will occasionally include an insert in the box so you can reorder more directly from the company, bypassing Amazon, and increasing the profit margin for the business on subsequent sales.

Bounceback offers are so successful that you'll find them in almost any industry. Even businesses like a dental office will schedule your next visit before you leave your current visit. They are locking in their next transaction with you *during* your current transaction. Why leave the follow up sale to chance?

This kind of bounceback doesn't even offer a promo or discount; it's merely offering a convenience so you can get your preferred appointment date and time six months out.

Even vacation destinations, like hotels, resorts, and cruise lines, famously incentivize you to book your next stay with *them* while you're *currently* staying with them. It's much easier to secure that next sale *during* the experience as opposed to *after*.

In all of these examples, the businesses know you're going to purchase again. It doesn't matter if it's needing more pens or dish detergent, or booking another vacation, or eating another meal out, you *will* buy again; they just want to make sure that next time the purchase is with *them* and not someone else.

So how do you make your bounceback offer effective?

- Make sure your offer is *relevant* to your target audience. It should be for the product or service that they already enjoyed and need again.

- Make sure your offer is easy to understand and redeem. Complexity will kill your sales. Your website, point of sale system, and staff need to know about and understand the offer.

- Deliver your offer *with* the purchase, i.e. in the box, in the thank you email, with the check, etc.

- Track the results of your offer so you can measure its effectiveness. You want to know if and how well it's working.

Put it into Action!

- What can you be doing to bring your customers back to *you* after purchase?

- When, where, and how will you offer your bounceback offer to your customers?

- Which of these strategies might fit your business model best?

Loyalty Programs

How else can businesses bring customers back again and again? One of our favorite strategies is using a loyalty program.

In its simplest form, this is like the punch card at your local coffee or ice cream shop. After ten visits or so, you get a free coffee or ice cream.

On the other end of the spectrum are things like credit cards with annual fees or high end club memberships with steep upfront fees and ongoing membership fees.

Programs such as airline frequent flyer programs fall somewhere in the middle.

Once you have "sunk cost" with a business and are making progress towards a reward with them... why would you, as a consumer, choose to spend your dollars with a different company?

Zappos, the multi-billion dollar shoe retailer that was bought by Amazon, has a hugely loyal customer base. And much of that has to do with their VIP program.

Their VIP program is the gold standard for customer loyalty in the world of ecommerce. Think of it as a super-fan club where members get treated like royalty. But it's not just about giving away free stuff; it's a strategic system *designed* to benefit both Zappos and their most valued customers.

But what makes this program so special? First off, it's free to join, which instantly makes it appealing to customers. Once they're in, the perks start rolling in. For example, all Zappos VIPs get free expedited shipping, so they don't have to pay for shipping or wait a long time for their new shoes.

And if something doesn't fit or a customer changes their mind, returns are simple - and completely free. Plus, Zappos has a dedicated customer service line just for VIPs, making members *feel* like they're getting the white-glove treatment.

That sounds expensive, but... is it?

Why is this model so good for Zappos?

Simply put, it keeps their VIP customers coming back for more. Loyal VIP members become a consistent revenue stream, spending more over time.

And the best part? It costs less to keep existing customers happy than to constantly hunt for new ones. Think of it as an investment in long-term relationships.

Plus, when your VIPs are happy, they become walking billboards for your brand. They rave about your amazing service and exclusive perks to their friends, family, and anyone who'll listen. It's free advertising! Word-of-mouth marketing is powerful, and we'll dig into that more in our chapter on Referrals.

Now, let's break down how the Zappos VIP program creates such a loyal following. It taps into a fundamental human desire: *the need to feel special.*

Everyone wants to be part of an exclusive club, and being a "VIP" definitely checks that box. But it's not just about the label; it's about the tangible benefits that make their shopping experience so much better. Free shipping, easy returns, and personalized attention – these are benefits that customers really value.

And then there's the gamified aspect of earning points. For every dollar spent, VIPs earn points that they can redeem for discounts and other goodies. It's like a treasure hunt that keeps them engaged and coming back for more.

Who doesn't love a good reward? It's a win-win situation; Zappos gets more sales, and customers get to treat themselves.

So, how can you, the savvy entrepreneur, use this model to create your own loyal customer base?

It's about understanding the *psychology* of loyalty and applying those principles to your specific business. Think about what your customers value the most and create a program that speaks to those desires.

Start by getting to know your audience inside and out.

What are their pain points? What makes them feel appreciated? (We get into this more in the exercise on your Your Ideal Customer)

Once you have a clear picture of what motivates them, you can start crafting a VIP program that resonates with their needs. Think of it as a personalized love letter to your most loyal customers.

Next, make it a journey, not just a destination.

A tiered system, like Zappos', is a great way to keep customers engaged and motivated to spend more. As they climb the VIP ladder, they unlock increasingly valuable benefits, turning their shopping experience into an exciting adventure.

This is like what the airline industry has used for decades. The more you fly, the better the benefits.

Cafés and ice cream shops have used simple paper punch cards for ages before making the transition to mobile wallet punch cards or dedicated mobile apps.

Starbucks, as an example, boasts over 27 *million* members in their loyalty program. And this kind of loyalty pays, as members typically buy *three times* more often as non-members.

And the revenue from members in their loyalty program?

Over *half* of their revenue comes from members!

Given the choice of visiting a non-Starbucks coffee shop - vs going out of the way to visit a Starbucks and earn points - members pick Starbucks.

Even the movie industry has gotten in on this game in recent years rewarding members for the number of movie tickets purchased during the year and offering tiered rewards based on money spent.

The more you spend or do, the closer you get to your next tier of membership benefits.

And remember, simplicity is key. Make joining and using your program easy. The last thing you want is to frustrate your customers with complicated rules (think "blackout dates" where you can't use membership benefits) or a clunky interface. The easier it is to participate, the more likely they are to stick around.

With Zappos, enrollment is as easy as signing up before purchase or being automatically enrolled after your first purchase.

What should you offer for rewards? Generic discounts - like 10% off, buy 10 get 1 free, etc - *do* work, but you can do so much better!

And - unlike the generic discounts that we warn against in our chapter on Decreasing the Amount of Each Transaction - these are rewards that customers earn by buying from you more frequently.

Get creative and offer perks that truly resonate with your customers. Think about offering exclusive experiences, early access to new products, or even personalized consultations.

The key is to make them feel like they're getting something truly special that they can't find anywhere else.

One of my clients, when implementing this strategy, went down the route of providing exclusive access to new products to his VIPs before the products went live online.

This first access benefit was so valuable to his VIP community. Even then, he'd almost always sell out of his initial small batches of product just amongst his VIPs.

Not only did this provide a benefit to his VIPs, but it got him early feedback and testimonials so that when he *did* launch his product online, it was dialed in and had social proof and reviews at launch.

As a closing thought on loyalty programs, remember that a loyalty program isn't just about *transactions*; it's also about building a community.

Foster a sense of belonging among your VIPs by hosting exclusive events, creating online forums or social media groups, and giving them opportunities to connect with each other and your brand.

We'll touch on events more in our section on Customer Appreciation Events.

When your VIPs feel like they're part of something special, their loyalty goes beyond just the punch card; they're part of something bigger.

Put it into Action!

- What could your loyalty program look like?

- What might you offer your customers for coming back to buy from you again and again?

- What kind of community can you create for your loyal repeat customers?

Consumables

In our chapter on Customer Lifetime Value (CLV), we told the story of Gillette and their razor blades. Their entire business was built around consumers coming back to buy another consumable.

Nowadays we see this model all around us from countertop sparkling water makers that require consumable and exclusive CO_2 cartridges to keep making fizzy water all the way to coffee makers that use pods.

Back in 1975, while working at Nestle, Éric Favre discovered how delicious coffee could be and set out to crack the code for making the perfect cup of coffee.

His research took him and his wife through Italy and Europe; what he found was much of the flavor came from the combination of oxygen with the beans.

But how can you keep that ratio perfect and controlled, yet shelf stable?

This led Eric to come up with an idea to prepackage "pods" of coffee with the right amount of oxygen so that when hot pressurized water was added... you'd get the perfect shot of espresso with *just* the right amount of crema on top.

Nestle corporate wanted nothing to do with the idea. Their fear was that by creating a coffee machine that used single use pods, they'd cannibalize their existing coffee maker market.

Not to be dissuaded, Eric persisted, and, by 1986, corporate finally came around and tested out the first Nespresso system.

The Nespresso system was an instant success, and it quickly became one of Nestle's most popular products. Favre's invention revolutionized the way people drink coffee, and it is now estimated that over *100 billion coffee pods are sold each year*!

Instead of cannibalizing Nestle's sales, the invention of the coffee pod *revolutionized* the coffee industry. It has made it easier and more convenient for people to enjoy a cup of coffee at home, and it has helped to create a new market for single-serve coffee products.

Once customers buy their Nespresso - or Keurig, etc - coffee machine, they continue to buy pods from the company for the life of that machine. That is a *massive* Frequency of Transactions!

Even something as "simple" as the book *The Five Minute Journal* fits this model. With millions upon millions of sold, its readers need to come back and buy it again and again as they fill in the pages of their journal.

And remember, the "book" is *mostly* blankish pages for journaling. But because of its unique structure, and beautiful introduction, it's able to command a premium retail price nearly twice as high as most any book that would sell just *once* to a consumer!

Customers value these consumables - from razor blades to coffee pods to journals. Their other option would be to pay more money up front for an expensive razor and then keep the blade sharpened. Or they'd have to buy a more expensive coffee maker and spend more time making coffee.

The consumable model still offers a value to the consumer over the alternative, and you can, too.

Put it into Action!

- What can you offer in your business that your customers would consume, get value from, and then need to buy from you *again*?

- What kind of consumables do other businesses in your space offer customers?

- How can you provide an alternative to your existing products for customers who want to spend less time using or caring for your product?

Repacking / Reformulating

On the topic of consumables, I've always enjoyed seeing how big name brands repackage their products for different markets. Something as simple as a box of ziptop food storage bags at a big box retailer like Target will be a different quantity than what you'd find at, say, Costco or Amazon.

It'll be the exact same product, but will *appear* cheaper at Target. Until you look and see that the *quantity* is less than what you'll find on Amazon. And then on the other end of the spectrum is a Costco, selling you the same thing at a *much* larger quantity.

So when you compare the actual *unit prices* - the cost per bag - you'll see that the unit price is often - but not always! - higher with a smaller quantity.

To the casual shopper looking at the price of plastic zip top bags, it'll be "cheaper" to buy the item at Target, but then they find themselves returning to buy more bags more frequently.

The manufacturer simply *repackaged* their product and created a different version of it at a higher per unit price and sold more units more often!

This isn't taking advantage of a customer. Instead, it's offering them the value that they're looking for: a lower overall price point or the right quantity of something.

And you can do the exact same thing.

Consider the story often attributed to shampoo companies marketing instructing people to not just rinse and lather, but to "rinse, lather, repeat" thereby using twice as much product and needing to repurchase twice as often.

Even Alka-Seltzer used this strategy to double their sales almost over night by suggesting that customers take two tablets instead of the previously suggested one.

The challenge that Alka Seltzer faced was that they had effectively tapped their addressable market and weren't seeing additional growth.

The marketing agency they were working with put out a commercial where the visual was simply two tablets dropping into a glass of water and frothing up. Note that it wasn't the one tab everyone had been taking; it was now two tabs.

The packaging team started putting two tables in a foil pouch and selling these everywhere so now consumers had two tabs at the ready each time they wanted to take Alka Seltzer.

And, no surprise, they nearly doubled their sales.

Comet, the household cleaner, faced a similar challenge. Comet was an abrasive cleaner for use around the home that came in a shaker tube, like parmesan cheese, with holes at the top. You shook it out like a spice jar, and then cleaned with it.

Having dominated the market and sold as much Comet as they could, Procter and Gamble couldn't figure out a way to increase sales.

The company demanded more sales; someone on the team had the bright idea of making the holes on the top of the package *bigger* so that each time someone shook it... *twice as much product would come out!*

In turn, consumers were buying the product twice as often.

What's important, though, is that customers continued to see the value in what they were buying. Had these companies gone too far or been dishonest, customers would no longer have valued what was being sold. In all of these cases, however, the consumer still found the repackaged products valuable.

Put it into Action!

- What can you change up in your product packaging that will bring customers back to buy more often?

- Could you offer a smaller unit count per package at a higher per unit cost?

- How might you change up the dosage or the amount of product used each time?

Sloanism - Ongoing Updates

By the year 1926, anyone who could afford an automobile typically had one. The entire addressable market had been addressed.

The following year, for the first time ever, both automobile manufacturing - and purchasing - was down for the first time *ever*.

This was what most would call a *problem* for the automotive industry.

Their challenge - and maybe you've felt something similar - was how to sell more cars if all the potential buyers *already had a car*?

Ford was known for making the same, reliable, single color choice, and durable Model T cars. Their customers didn't need to replace them. The cars worked just fine, looked good, and did their job.

Just like your countertop stand mixer. It does the job, lasts a long time, and looks good.

Alfred Sloan, president of General Motors at the time, took a different approach from Ford.

Under his leadership, GM started releasing an updated newer model of their cars each year.

Think body refresh, new features, superficial updates, performance improvements, and more.

Suddenly, even though you had a perfectly usable car at home, you started comparing it to the latest models coming out and became increasingly dissatisfied with what you already had.

New cars became a status symbol, and existing car owners were suddenly buyers of the latest model cars once again.

Sloan's approach meant that "one-off" GM customers came back to buy again; the media and market had something to talk about (what was "new"), and they were now clearly different from Ford, which was thus automatically positioned as old and outdated.

This model has been used in another industry-defining way in far more recent history, too.

Before the advent of Software as a Service (SaaS), which we covered early in the chapter, software was sold for a one-time fee. Software manufacturers would work all year long on updates.

At times, some of these software updates were not even backwards compatible, meaning that once one computer was upgraded, other computers without the newer software wouldn't be able to access files created by the computers using the latest version of the software. Now customers had a reason to come back and buy the software that they already owned again.

Even though what they had was perfectly fine.

Add on to that the network effect of, for example, someone sending you a file in a newer format that your older software couldn't read.

Now you almost *had* to pay to buy the software again just to get a compatible version to what everyone else was using.

Maybe you have a product that, once purchased, never needs replacement. You're not alone in facing that challenge to customers buying again. This strategy can solve for that.

Clients of mine have used this exact strategy in the software space with annual repurchases or license sales from existing customers.

They've continued to add value through their ongoing updates which is why customers continue to purchase seemingly the same thing again.

And you can, too.

Put it into Action!

- What can you update in *your* product or service that would bring past customers back again to buy *the same thing, just newer* because of what you've added since they last bought?

- What updates would make their previous purchase pale in comparison to your *new and improved* version?

- How have customer wants and needs changed since you last released your product?

Customer Appreciation Events

If you have a physical business - or an opportunity to connect with your global customers more regionally, like at an industry tradeshow or road-show - hosting a customer appreciation event is not only a great way to show your customers some love, it's a chance for them to re-engage with your business and buy again.

A company I was working with was in the B2B Software as a Service (SaaS) space and loved doing these kinds of events; because they *worked*.

As they'd attend and sponsor tradeshows and events where their customers were in attendance, they'd host customer appreciation events at a local restaurant to connect with the customers and referral partners. (See our chapter on Affiliates / Partners).

This was not only great for relationships, but it was also a chance for existing customers to meet businesses like theirs, learn how they were using the SaaS platform, and in turn expand their own usage of the product by upgrading their plan, adding more users/seats, and so on.

Costs were minimal, as it was basically just paying the restaurant for food and drink. Marketing was free - and warm - as it was internal to existing customers and partners. But the payoff, connection, and relationship time was high.

These events reenergized and reengaged partners. They facilitated valuable facetime with clients and partners. And attendees had *fun*.

Even cooler was the fact that attendees had a chance to get to know *each other* where the commonality and shared interest was their relationship with the company. This was much easier networking and connecting than would happen at a large trade show on its own.

Another client was in the high end portrait photography business and put together a customer appreciation event for past clients and referral partners to get together and party.

Not only was it great networking, all of the attendees were super fans. During the event, most all that anyone was saying was that they realized it'd been too long since their last portraits, and it was time to get updated portraits.

These were all past clients who had already bought.

Only by seeing the newly updated studio, portraits on display, and other clients, did they come to realize how long it'd been since their last shoot, and how it was time to schedule their next session.

The cost to host the event - just as above - was just food and beverage.

Another client was opening a new retail location for her business; it was going to be a new business in a neighboring market.

By setting up a customer appreciation event at the *new* location, past customers were able to not just see what was new, but also make purchases while in store. And then of course, tell their friends about the new location.

In all of these cases, attendees enjoyed the intimacy of a smaller VIP event, made great connections, felt honored and loved, got wonderful facetime with the business and business owner, and spent more.

Just by showing your customers some love and appreciation, many will naturally transact again, increasing your Frequency of Transactions.

Put it into Action!

- What kind of exclusive invite only Customer Appreciation event could you host for your past and existing clients?

- What would entice your existing and past clients to attend your event and bring a friend or two?

- How will you make the event an experience to remember that attendees will talk about for years to come?

Strategies for Reducing Churn

Now that you know how important reducing churn is, from our chapter on Customer Lifetime Value (CLV), what can we do to reduce our churn?

Through working with hundreds of subscription-based businesses, I've found that subscription cancellations are usually for one of four major reasons, which we'll get to shortly.

At the root of it, you need to continue to provide value to your members if you want to keep them paying month after month.

Value can come in the form of delivering great content, providing a great return on the monthly investment, providing continual access to valuable resources, and more.

When members do decide to cancel, what kind of cancellation system do you have in place?

Do you have a system to find out why your members are cancelling?

Do you have offers to keep your members with you, perhaps at a higher or lower membership level that would better suit their needs?

The business run by Damien, one of my clients, was all about membership - on the backend.

New customers would come onboard by purchasing his product, and then have an opportunity to enroll in an add-on membership program at an additional cost beyond the initial purchase.

Not only was he getting the upfront transaction, but he was more often than not getting customers to agree to repeat transactions right after purchase.

This was an effective upsell that provided ongoing monthly revenue and increased both the dollar amount of his initial transactions and the frequency of customer transactions.

He even delivered great value and members that *used* their membership loved it. Sometimes, though, members *did* want to cancel their account.

That's only natural, and may happen to you, too.

Knowing this, and knowing the four reasons why members cancel, we were able to put a strategy in place to reduce churn.

So, what are our four major categories of cancellation? Why do members cancel?

- No Money - the customer can't afford the membership

- No Time - the customer doesn't have time to use the membership

- No Value - the customer has the time and money but doesn't think it's worthwhile

- Too Complicated - the customer has the time, money, and sees the value, but finds the membership too complicated to use

Believe it or not, there are *solutions* to all four of these cancellation reasons, and if you address them, you can save your customer cancellations.

This all starts with a customer inquiry, though, and ends with how your support team handles the cancellation request.

In Damien's case, he found that when a customer wanted to cancel, with the right cancellation system in place, he was able to "save" many of his cancellations and keep his customers with his business longer, getting more value for their time and money.

It all comes down to having the right *system* in place for his team to use.

We created an email template for Damien's team to use, one each for the cancellation reasons that he'd hear from his customers.

Depending on the reason for the cancellation, there was one of four "Save Offers" available for his team to use, for example, changing the customer's membership level, upgrading them to a higher package, downgrading them to lower cost option, sending them a free gift, and more.

We even went so far as to create a special webpage - one for each of these reasons - and put a video on each page with the save offer delivered from the heart.

The email templates said that Damien totally understood the reason for the cancellation and invited the customer to view Damien's special message.

It was deeply personal, from the heart, and high touch.

This system we put in place for Damien allowed his team to not only work efficiently, but also provide more value to his customers, *and* it meant he kept more of his business' hard earned memberships with him longer.

Keep in mind that this isn't about having a "retention" department, aggravating customers who want to cancel, or making it difficult for them. It's about *understanding* why a customer wants to cancel and *offering* a solution to that problem.

Many customers may still want to cancel, and that's *okay*. But for the ones who *do* take you up on a save offer... you've helped them *and* kept a customer with you longer.

Put it into Action!

- How could you better track *why* your customers are cancelling and discover their unmet needs?

- What offers could you put in place in your business for each of these 4 cancellation categories?

- How can you empower your team to help customers stay with you when they *do* request to cancel?

As we've seen, Increasing the Frequency of Transactions with your new and existing customers is one of my favorite places to start when working with clients. These are often the "lowest hanging fruits" that can yield quick wins.

But this is only the first of the three big levers you have in your business! In the next section we'll get into your second lever, increasing the Amount of Each Transaction.

Increasing the Amount of Each Transaction

"To sell well is to convince someone else to part with resources - not to deprive that person, but to leave him better off in the end." - Daniel Pink

You're familiar with the classic "Would you like fries with that?" upsell from McDonalds. Because it works.

There are a dozen ways to increase the amount of each transaction, but your two easiest ones to implement – today – are Upsells and Increasing Your Prices.

Upsells / Add-Ons

McDonalds' margin on a double cheeseburger is about 55% on a good day, but their profit margin on fries is a staggering 75-90%!

If you were McDonalds, you'd want to sell more fries, too.

This is why when they serve over 69 *million* people every *day* around the globe they offer their classic upsell of "Would you like fries with that?"

That helps them to sell over *9 million pounds* of their profit rich signature french fries every single *day*.

You don't need to run a business the size of McDonalds to incorporate upsells like theirs into your business, too.

Adding an Upsell is simply having an additional add-on offer with each of your transactions. Think how retail stores always have grabbable impulse buy items at the counter: gum, magazines, candy, and so on.

These all increase the dollar amount of the transaction.

This works with other business models, too.

A training and education business we were working with had pivoted from selling a box course for learning at home to selling tickets to a live event instead.

Not surprisingly, people learn a lot more in a room all together where they can focus on the content, ask their questions, and connect with other students.

The live event was also a much higher end experience than just learning on your own at home and so cost more than the physical course. That *value* was much higher.

On the expense side, the physical course was almost all profit margin as the only cost of goods were printing, fulfillment, and shipping. A live event, however, was outrageously expensive, from rooms to AV, to staff, to hotel contracts, to food, and more.

Changing from a physical box course to a live event was effectively a price increase as tickets were $1,497 per attendee. So that pivot already increased the *amount* of the initial transaction.

Additionally, one of the other benefits of live events is that once students were there in the room, there were some additional opportunities to buy from guest speakers teaching niche content in the room.

This increased the *frequency* of transactions beautifully.

But how about increasing the *amount* of the transaction even further?

Well, implementing this Upsell strategy, we added in at first one additional upsell, and in the end three upsells in total during the checkout flow of the initial event registration. And all of the upsells were high margin.

The result was that, on average, we saw every person checking out took us up on 1 additional high profit upsell.

While some registrants didn't take any upsells, many registrants took advantage of *all three* upsells!

This same upsell strategy works in most any reputable e-commerce shopping cart platform.

Simply look at your existing sales funnel and add in an upsell offer at the time of transaction – whether in person or online.

Back to the car wash example in our chapter on Subscriptions, think about how, when you get to a car wash, you can pay for one wash now, or... for a higher price you can become a monthly car wash member...

You were just upsold to a higher amount – that has more value and has a recurring transaction.

That one upsell offer increased BOTH the Frequency and the Amount!

An estate planning attorney client had a traditional estate planning practice of getting paid a flat fee for an estate plan and ending up with a one-time "once and done" transaction with a client until they passed away.

At which point he *might* - but often would not - get a call for a possible second transaction.

One of the biggest challenges for folks who get estate plans, though, is that they often fall out of date. Despite establishing a trust to hold ones assets, not all assets are always put into the trust.

And then, over time, as assets are bought and sold, the trust is rarely kept current.

This then defeats much of the purpose of the trust, as all the items outside of the trust then typically have to go through the usual probate process, which can be slow, time consuming, and costly.

Changing things up for the industry, this attorney pivoted and - in addition to offering an annual continuity program to keep an estate plan up to date with clients - added that continuity program on as an upsell at the initial transaction.

Now, when clients came in to make what was classically a one-time transaction, they were paying a higher Amount *and* increasing the Frequency of their transactions.

How many times have you had a shopping cart full online and started to check out, only to see an offer of free shipping if your order hits a certain amount?

The offer of free shipping entices buyers to add *more* to their cart - often things they weren't looking for in the first place - just to get the free shipping. This upsell does exactly what it intended - it increased the Amount of the transaction. We'll dive more into this category of tactic on Tiered Bonuses.

Upsells can sometimes be called add-ons, and while they serve the same purpose, they're often used in different ways.

One common challenge that scaling businesses have when they have too many leads or customers is that operations can't keep up on fulfillment. This causes bottlenecks further down the line in the business, and for a services based business, can sometimes mean scheduling new clients out weeks to months.

That may sound like a good problem to have, and in some ways it is. But some prospects will decide not to work with you because of the delay to get started.

Adding in an expedite fee can help those clients with more urgent needs "skip to the front of the line" and get started with you earlier.

One of our clients offered high end design services and was facing just this challenge. So they used this strategy, first offering a four-figure expedite fee.

And... almost every single one of their new clients took them up on it!

When everyone says "yes" to the expedite fee, it doesn't solve the bottleneck problem.

The next step was to bump the fee up to five figures and keep adjusting until they had some - but not all - clients taking them up on the fee.

Without this fee, not only were they leaving money on the table, they were losing prospective clients!

One of my earlier businesses, that I got out of quickly, resold computer hardware - which classically has terrible margins. All the real money came from the service side. When customers bought our hardware, we'd offer install and setup services, which was almost all profit. Selling the hardware was really a *means* to sell the high margin service!

And... like many of our tactics, this one small add-on had the side effect of increasing the Quantity of Transactions, too, because it closed more sales since customers didn't need to figure out how to install on their own!

This installation / setup fee model doesn't just apply to computer hardware. We've used this successfully in SaaS businesses for paid customer training and onboarding, appliance companies use this for delivery and install fees, home security companies use this for installation, and more.

The important distinction here is that none of these are junk fees that annoy customers. These are *optional* fees that new customers *can* happily pay to increase the *value* of their initial purchase.

In other words, if the fee you're charging is *required* or a customer *can't* do business with you without paying that fee, then it's not an upsell or an add-on.

Put it into Action!

- What optional upsells and add-ons can you put into your sales process that would offer more value to a segment of your customers?

- Would you be able to offer an expedite, priority, or rush fee for clients that want to "skip the line" and get service sooner?

- What do your customers have to do now when they purchase from you that you could offer to do for them or with them to provide more value?

While you can certainly increase the cart total with additional items and upsells, there's another even easier way to increase the Amount of your transactions.

And that's... simply increasing your prices.

Increasing Your Prices

Increasing Your Prices comes with two big challenges. The first is mental. The other is strategic.

Strategically, if you're selling a commodity and you feel "I can't charge more or my customer will just get the same thing somewhere else", you're in what authors W. Chan Kim and Renée Mauborgne call a "Red Ocean" in their aptly named best selling book *Blue Ocean Strategy*.

Differentiate your business so there's no more competition, and bask in your "blue ocean" where you can increase your pricing.

Most of that comes down to niching, specialization, branding, and increasing the value that you offer.

Remember it's not about if *you* think there's any competition. This is about your prospective customers *perceiving* you to have competition - and them having alternatives.

So your first step is to make sure there is no *perceived* competition.

Now when your customers don't see there being any viable alternatives to your product or service, you can increase pricing, and ideally your value as well.

So what stops most businesses from increasing their prices?

Mentally, you likely have some head trash around increasing your prices.

Most business owners like you do.

You know what you've always charged, and have set the value there for yourself. Good news: you're worth more! You are allowed to increase your prices unapologetically!

Even if you're in a business with pricing contracts, you can simply build in price increases. This is now a standard clause in many longer term contracts to avoid renegotiation or having an uncomfortable conversation in the future. Just build in a set increase each year.

Another client I was working with had built from scratch - with lots of mistakes and learning along the way - a successful small business that quickly got to generating six figures a year with just the owner running the business part-time.

A client of hers reached out and asked if she'd be willing to fly out and teach them how she started her business so they could do the same thing. Naturally, the topic of pricing came up.

How do you price teaching someone all of your best practices so they can avoid the same mistakes you learned the hard way and implement the shortcuts you painstakingly found?

This business owner thought about what she thought her time was worth, and then took into account the cost of her flights and accommodations and other related travel expenses, and didn't love how little she'd be making.

"Why are you basing this on some hourly rate?" I asked.

She hadn't thought to price it any other way and so we got into a discussion around *value* based pricing.

"What's the *value* in this client downloading your playbook from you, which shows how to launch a six-figure business like yours?" I continued.

"What would someone be willing to pay to know what you know and repeat what you did to launch your business?"

In the end, we added a zero to the price she was going to propose. Yes, we 10xed her original time based pricing by moving to value based pricing.

Oh, and the travel expenses? That became the responsibility of the client and not an expense for her.

But how do you get a higher price when you're still mentally stuck at a lower valuation?

For starters, and this may feel silly, practice presenting your price in the mirror. Roleplay it. When you can say your pricing without laughing, puking, or stuttering, you're most of the way there!

Now that's for a service based business. What about for a product based business or Software as a Service based business?

This is often as easy as simply clicking into your sales page or CRM, editing your pricing, and moving on with your day.

In a previous subscription-based business of mine, we hemmed and hawed about raising our pricing.

A member of a Mastermind Group we were in shared how he had increased his subscription pricing and didn't lose any customers, and in fact started to attract more customers.

Even if that was the case for his business, what if it wasn't the case for ours? What if we lost customers due to the price increase? Or we enrolled fewer new customers because of the higher pricing?

Look at what the difference in your pricing will be and do some math.

Let's say you have a $40/mo subscription program. And you want to increase the pricing to $50/mo. That's a 25% increase. (50-40 = $10. $10/40 = 25%.) That means you *could* afford to lose around 25% of your customers and still be better off.

"Better off how?" you ask?

Say you have 1,000 subscribers at $40/mo. That's $40,000/mo in gross revenue. Say you increase the pricing to $50/mo. If you lose 20% of your customers because of the change, you're still making the same gross (800*$50 = 1,000*$40), but your *profit* is higher.

Let's say your expenses and cost to service a customer all in is $30/mo/customer so your profit was $10/mo. Increasing your pricing *doubles* your profit for all the customers that stay with you.

So even with the $40,000/mo gross staying the same and you *losing* 200 customers, your profit would go from $10,000/mo to $16,000/mo.

Put it into Action!

- How much more could you increase your prices?

- What would it take for you to "try it out" and see how increased pricing impacts sales?

- Is it just a matter of updating a sales page or an order form? Changing the number on a marketing piece? What's the quickest / fastest / easiest way you can test out increased pricing?

The Power of Niching

If you needed specialized open heart surgery, would you want to go to a general practitioner family doctor? Or would you want to go to the best cardiac surgeon available?

You want the specialist.

And the more specialized a product or service, the more valuable it is - and the more it can cost.

It's not unusual for a business to niche down its offerings and in turn not only win more business as a specialist but also command a much higher price because of it.

If you've had the pleasure of planning a wedding, you've seen this first hand. The cost of a wedding venue and its associated fees is multitudes higher than more generic venues. Talk to a hotel about a ballroom for a private event vs. a wedding and you'll see the difference in costs!

A dedicated wedding venue that does nothing but weddings can easily sell against a more generic location that *also* does weddings. And that specialization is worth a *lot* to the buyer.

One of our clients had a firm specializing in business valuations and business brokerage. They were successful across a wide range of industries, but three particular industries made up a larger portion of their portfolio.

Instead of positioning themselves as generic business brokers who did valuations for any business, we worked with them to dial in their positioning specifically for those top three industries.

Instead of showing *breadth* of experience to a niche industry prospect, they instead showed *depth* of experience.

A few small tweaks to their outgoing call scripts, email templates, and pitch deck made all the difference. Suddenly instead of trying to speak to *any* business, they were using the *language* of the niche, case studies and examples *only* in that niche, images that spoke to that niche, and more.

And of course, now that they were marketing themselves as a specialist in that niche, they could command a much higher price for the same work they were already doing.

There's truth in the phrase "Riches in Niches."

And remember, just because you specialize in a certain niche, nobody is saying you have to turn down business outside of that area. You can still take that business. You just better attract those *in* the niche and can command a higher price.

You also don't have to pick just one niche and rebuild your entire company around that. From the largest and most complex company to the simplest, you can alternatively have:

- Specialized brands under your company that target individual niches.

- Departments that specialize in each niche.

- Landing pages and sales copy that speak to each niche.

- Offers and packages for each niche.

Put it into Action!

- How can you specialize what you're already offering to a certain niche and solve their unique challenges?

- Could you set up a dedicated landing page just for that niche? Register a new domain name and build a microsite entirely focused on that niche?

- Could you update your emails and sales material to target that one niche?

Bundling for Profit

Beyond just upsells and add-ons, another favorite tactic of ours is to leverage bundles at check-out.

This specific technique comes down to you grouping other products and services of yours together to sell as a bundle.

A company we were working with ran a number of live in-person events during the month with guest speakers that came in and presented to attendees.

Beyond just generating revenue from the live events, we also had them record the presentations, which were then transcribed, summarized, and sold after the fact. So, even if you missed the live event, you could still buy a copy of the audio, transcript, and highlights.

We then bundled these up by topic so that, when customers went to buy one of them, we could upsell them to a bundle on the same topic.

And keep in mind that these were very high margin sales. All it cost was a physical CD with audio on it and a few sheets of paper. Adding on anything in a bundle increased not just gross sales, but profitability, too.

Book publishers do this, too, when you go to purchase one book in a series, the natural bundle is to offer you the entire series of books.

Now bundling typically works best if you have a catalog of related products, but... there's another way to get there, too!

You can also bundle other businesses' products, too! This gets them new customers (more Q) to try out their products *and* can generate more revenue for you (more A).

One example of this model is at the core of a little company called Humble Bundle. Launched in 2010 as a way to sell *other* game developers games - with none of their own - they've grown to over 12 *million* customers and donated over $265 *million* to great causes.

You have likely experienced this with your mobile provider, too. When you get service with them - at a higher price than their competitors - they'll give you - or discount for you - the physical phone.

Event organizers can do a great job of this as well. One of our clients was putting on a high end in-person event. In addition to all of the normal "swag bag" items included with the event registration that you get at the check in table, they also included books from each of the authors and experts who were in attendance and speaking. At each of the breaks between the guest speakers' TED Talk style presentations, the event team would come around and deliver the next round of books to every table.

Thoughtfully, one of the included pieces of event swag was a soft duffle bag as when the event was over, each attendee had a bag bursting with a bookshelf worth of books to bring home. And these were books by authors that each of the attendees had a chance to spend the past few days with. The value was *huge*, not just to the event attendees, but to each of the authors, *and* to the event organizer.

All of this because of bundling.

Authors even use this external-product strategy, too, when launching their books. When prospective buyers go to order their book directly, they can upgrade to a *bundle* that includes a ton of bonuses from *other* partner companies, too!

The bundle is what increases the value and allows you to charge more, often without increasing your costs or cutting into your profits.

Put it into Action!

- What can you bundle together in your product catalog for your buyers?

- What future content might you create – from live training recordings to podcast episodes to online courses – that could then be bundled?

- What partner businesses could you create bundles with?

Cross Selling "Across the Aisle"

We covered Upsells at the start of this chapter, and we'll get into Downsells in the next chapter, but there is a related strategy called a *Cross Sell*.

So how do Cross Sells differ?

A cross sale is an offer of a complementary product to what your customer is already purchasing. Something you added from our strategy of Expanding Your Product Portfolio in the previous chapter.

Now, instead of just using those new products to increase the Frequency of Transactions during launch by offering them to your *existing* customer base, you move the offer window up to the time of purchase for your *new* (and returning) customers.

Unlike Upsells and Add-Ons in the previous chapter, which are typically directly related to the purchase the customer is making – think back to the VIP upgrades, add on sessions, and fries mentioned – a Cross Sell serves the same audience but doesn't have much else to do with the *existing* purchase.

E-commerce businesses often do this with their automated carousel during checkout of "Customers who purchased X also purchased Y."

Gas stations do this beautifully as well, offering everything a driver or passenger could need while stopped for gas: From hot food, to coffee, to snacks, carwash, oil, and more. They're all cross sold purchases you can make while making your primary purchase of more fuel.

A locksmithing business client of ours even got into the world of cross selling to increase the Amount of each transaction. Typically, new commercial customers were reaching out to the locksmiths for access control systems, like badge scanner systems and door locks.

But customers who need access control may also want to *monitor* their security as well. Which fits in beautifully with camera and security systems. That's an entirely *different* product line, solving an entirely *different* problem, but was a common need for the same *category* of customers.

By adding these camera systems into new customer orders, the order size increased considerably.

We even went one step further to include these camera system questions into the sales process so sales reps were trained to *ask* about the existing security system and *offer* a security system to be put in at the time of install.

In one study, McKinsey looked at how customers "crossed the aisle" to buy a different category of products than what they were shopping for. What they found was that, depending on the category the customer was purchasing, the impact on their CLV varied. (See the chapter on Your Ideal Customer)

For example, toy buying customers dramatically increased their CLV when offered products across the aisle, but pet supply buyers barely bought anything else.

However... right between those two extreme categories of customers, they found the sweet spot of categories (sports and fitness, garden, and pharmacy, for example) where spend could be reliably increased through cross selling.

In fact, they found that the simple cross sell strategy increased sales by 20% - and profits by 30%!

Put it into Action!

- Which of the additional products that you have - or added on - can you start to offer to your customers at their time of purchase?

- What other categories of offers can you help your customers purchase "across the aisle"?

- Which segment of your customer base might be your "Hyper Buyers" that would be most receptive to cross sells?

Be the Bank with Payment Plans

One of the reasons your buyers might "tap out" and not take you up on a higher priced offering is simply... the price.

Higher price points - especially when you're actively increasing the Amount of the transaction like we're doing in this chapter - can often be overcome with a payment plan option.

Basically, you get to be the bank and split the payments up for your buyer.

Payment plans *typically* come at a cost for the buyer, but you can also offer to split payments without a "fee".

For example, if you're increasing the cost of your product from $1,500 to, say, $2,000, you might present that as *"two payments of $1,000 or $1,900 if paid in full today."*

This gets you a higher ticket sale, and optionally "costs" the customer $100 more to pay in two installments. This isn't interest or a finance charge or anything complicated. It's merely a different payment agreement.

From another perspective, paying in full simply nets your customer a *discount*.

You can of course split a sale into more payments than just two; just be mindful of the administrative overhead of more payments, and the ensuing collection efforts for any missed payments.

Your e-commerce platform can easily handle the setup of a "multi-pay" agreement on any order, complete with recurring billing, automated emails in case of card decline, etc.

A client of mine was selling an online certification course and wanted to boost her prices. Just like we advise. As she did so, increasing the course enrollment fee to $5,000, she offered a two pay option for prospective students.

They simply had to put a $2,500 deposit down today to secure their spot in the class, and then pay the balance the following month.

This both let the students spread the cost out *and* lowered the cost to get started.

There was no extra cost to splitting the payments, it just helped to increase conversions. Which is a double win as not only did more students enroll in the course, the enrollment was *also* higher!

This works best on "soft" goods with high profit margins as any missed payments just cut into profit, and don't incur any actual hard costs for you because, yes, some customers may default on their second payment and it will remain uncollected.

And a note on when to start and complete your payment plans... sooner is better. There should be a payment up front before delivery, and the next payment no more than a month out.

I've had clients run product launches with payment plans that didn't start until a year after purchase and you can imagine what a mess that was. Not only do cards expire and get cancelled, customers who aren't even using the service a year later may not even remember who you are or what they signed up for. Don't do that.

In addition to multi-pays allowing you to increase the Amount of a Transaction, they also help you to increase the Quantity of your Transactions, too!

Put it into Action!

- Which of your products/services could use a price increase partnered with a multi-pay option?

- How might you structure your multi-pay options? Two payments? Three payments? Half up front?

- What will you do to incentivize and reward customers who opt to pay in full?

Third Party Financing Partners

What if you don't want to be the bank and your customer doesn't want to finance their purchase with their credit card?

This is where third party financing companies come in!

Typically without even a credit check, a third party company will "underwrite" the risk of financing a purchase, and then pay you out in (almost) full at the time of purchase.

As an example, let's say you have a $7,000 course that you're selling. A customer wants to purchase your course, but doesn't want to pay in full or put that all on their credit card right now. They simply complete a short application with your financing partner who then pays you, say, $6,500 immediately, and you have a new customer!

The financing partner takes care of collecting payments, handling missed payments, and even dealing with write offs of any debt they can't collect.

It's a beautiful way to facilitate a higher end sale and get a new customer immediately without taking on the billing, admin, follow up, collections, or possible write offs.

We've successfully used this many times, often at live events where higher end programs are sold. The financing company has one of their representatives at the sales table, or at the table one over, and helps close any deals where the higher price point is an issue.

This works for smaller purchases, too!

PayPal found that when small businesses offered their "Buy Now Pay Later" program to prospective customers that sales increased 6%! And that was at *no cost* to the business!

Even better, customers who used their Buy Now Pay Later ("BNPL") program, spent around 30% *more* than other buyers.

Those are both fantastic for increasing not just the Amount of the Transaction, but the Quantity of Transactions, too!

Put it into Action!

- How could you integrate financing options with a financing partner?

- If customers didn't need to pay for your entire product or service up front, by how much would you increase your prices?

- Which BNPL provider will you partner with to offer this kind of financing to your buyers?

Tiered Bonuses by Purchase Amount

At the start of the chapter, I touched on how free shipping encourages customers to add more to their cart to get free shipping.

That's just one of many ways of offering what I call *Tiered Bonuses* to encourage a higher spend.

How well do tiered bonuses work, though?

Let's stick with free shipping and find out. Studies have shown that a free shipping offer at a certain spend tier can increase spend by 30%! That's a BIG improvement to the A in your FAQ equation!

Even better, Shopify (and a Baymard study) found that a free shipping offer reduced cart abandonment by 20-30%. Which is a great way to increase your Quantity, too!

Other common ways of offering tiered bonuses include offering a free gift with a purchase above a certain amount.

Retail stores famously provide free gifts with purchases, whether it's a free gift with a $50 purchase, a gift card with a $100 purchase, a free HDMI cable with certain TVs, free personalization / monogram with purchases over a certain amount, free pair of socks with purchase, free sheets to go with certain mattresses, etc.

The bonus doesn't just need to be a gift, though. It can be an additional service like an extended warranty, or free service visit.

The goal is the same, regardless of *what* the bonus is: for your customers to spend more to get the tiered bonus.

Put it into Action!

- What could you offer as a free gift or bonus as your customers hit certain order amounts?

- What else can you offer that has a low cost to you but a high perceived value to your customers?

- Will you have just one bonus at a certain spend or will you offer multiple tiers of bonuses?

Customization / Personalization

From custom "vanity" license plates, to team numbers and names on t-shirts, to unique car colors, to personalized engraving on your Apple purchases, buyers are willing to pay premiums to make something *theirs*.

Given the opportunity to personalize their purchase, many customers will do just that.

Some businesses are even built entirely around this concept.

One of our clients printed bespoke children's books that put the buyer (or more commonly their gift recipient) *into* the story. Beyond just buying a good book, the buyer was getting a *personalized* keepsake, worth far more than an off the shelf book.

Often making your entire experience, product, or service bespoke allows you to differentiate from the competition *and* charge a premium.

When you purchase your devices directly from Apple, you can often have them custom engraved with initials, emojis, names, or quotes. For free. And only direct from Apple.

Buying your Apple devices from retailers, big box stores, or online e-commerce sites may be cheaper - but buying from Apple directly has a huge value add.

Not only do you get the custom personalization, which is a huge value add for you as the buyer, Apple makes far more profit by selling direct to consumer vs. through a retailer.

While our family was traveling through Spain, we wanted to take our kids to see a Flamenco show. While there were many options, only one production seemed to be really family friendly with earlier kid-friendly show times. They had stellar reviews, too.

When we arrived, we were greeted by name, given complimentary drinks on the way to our seats, and found a custom welcome screen awaiting us, greeting us by name.

It was an over the top WOW experience - and worth the premium paid for the personal experience.

And you can offer this exact same kind of wow experience to your buyers, too.

Put it into Action!

- What customization or personalization can you offer your buyers at the time of purchase?

- How can your customers differentiate their purchase from anyone else's purchase?

- What kind of personalized experience can you offer at purchase or during delivery / fulfillment?

Volume Discounts for Quantity

What do you sell that customers buy more of later on?

How can you sell *more* of what you sell at the time of purchase?

An e-commerce client of ours implemented this exact strategy when prospects would respond to a lead gen offer for a supplement sample pack.

The lead magnet offer was for a free small sample, all the buyer had to do was pay for shipping and handling. But at that point the first-time customer was already buying a small quantity... they already valued the product.

So a volume offer was put in to buy a regular sized pack of the product - and even a third option for a multipack at a discount.

This took an upfront purchase that had no to negative profit margin (but still got a customer that bought more in time with CLV) and made their initial transaction not only larger... but also more profitable.

Promotional product ("swag") and printing companies classically do this, too. The more of an item you buy, the cheaper it is. These are commonly called "price breaks".

Next thing you know, customers are buying more than they need to get a better price.

Even selling products like this book have volume discount opportunities for buyers. Encouraging a buyer to go from buying one book for themselves, to buying a quantity of books for their team, or a large volume for their entire conference is transformative.

An event company we were working with was selling individual tickets to attend their events. One of the first upsells we put in was an offer to bring a +1 for a reduced price.

This could be a business partner, a spouse, a colleague, a friend, it didn't matter. The point was that a customer already buying could easily get double what they were paying for a discount.

Even better, the more attendees physically in the room, the better the event was overall, and the more profitable it was.

Another client used this strategy when selling to parents.

Simply asking which other kids in the family should be enrolled with a sibling discount increased enrollment!

The cost to acquire your new customer is fixed, no matter how much they buy up front. You might as well help your customers to buy more volume at the time of purchase.

Put it into Action!

- How can you sell a higher quantity of what you are already selling at the time of purchase?

- Why might a buyer need more than one of what you're selling?

- What would incentivize your buyers to purchase more up front?

Prepaid Options for Recurring Sales

If you sell a recurring subscription service - like SaaS, a membership site, etc - allowing your customers to *prepay* for a period of time at purchase is a great way of increasing your initial sale price.

Especially if you know your churn, and when customers typically cancel, you can dial in the prepay period to go beyond that.

For example, let's say you know that most of your members stay with you for six months. Offering a nine-month prepay is *already* keeping them with you longer than they normally would.

Most SaaS platforms, on their pricing or signup page by default show the monthly pricing *when paid for upfront annually*. Toggling to paying monthly increases the monthly pricing.

With anchoring set at the discounted monthly price, most SaaS buyers (over 65%!) prepay annually instead of paying more monthly.

You still always have monthly available for cash strapped buyers, or those who would prefer to manage cashflow differently, so you don't *lose* any customers by offering the annual prepay.

You do, however, get over your churn hump, increase the Amount of the initial transaction, and increase your CLV.

As for the accounting and technical side of things, the billing complexities of customers upgrading, downgrading, changing their billing term, and all, can easily be handled by most self-service billing systems.

And remember, this strategy is used by far more businesses than just SaaS.

This is used successfully for membership sites, digital content providers, print media companies, wellness services, drop shipping subscription box companies, and more.

Even tutoring business clients of ours have successfully used this simple strategy moving clients from paying for individual tutoring sessions, to paying by the week, month, and quarter up front.

Two important notes if you go this route of offering annual subscriptions...

First, make sure that you proactively notify your customers ahead of their longer term renewals!

Customers on monthly renewals, when they forget to cancel, generally understand if you don't refund their recent monthly renewal. And worst case if you do decide to refund their recent renewal because they notified you shortly after the renewal, you're only out for one month's fee.

When a customer reaches out because of a charge on their card for an entire upcoming *year*, they expect a full refund. This not only dampens your cashflow, it messes with your cash forecasting, *and* also *costs* you quite a bit as you have to pay processing fees for the renewal and the refund.

So, as a best practice, leading up to an annual renewal, reach out with a reminder of what they're getting, how wonderful it is, how much they're paying, when you will be charging them, and what card you plan to be billing.

The second issue with annual renewals is credit card expirations. Most cards are issued with an expiration date three to four years out, meaning that in any given year, over 25% of your cards on file for annual renewals will have expired. And that doesn't include the cards that were cancelled or replaced!

This is easily solved, though, as your CRM or billing system should be able to see upcoming card expirations and proactively reach out to customers to update their card on file *before* it expires.

Only send these credit card expiration notices to customers with *active* subscriptions billing on the expiring card. In other words, don't hassle customers with expiring cards that aren't going to be billed!

This is a best practice for monthly *and* annual billing, but is especially problematic with annual renewals.

One last technical note on this: some credit card processors will even proactively update an expiring credit card with its new expiration date for you without you having to do anything.

This service called "card updater" or "account updater" allows the card networks - like Visa and Mastercard - to proactively update the card when it's replaced due to theft or reissued due to expiry.

Put it into Action!

- When do your recurring customers typically churn?

- What period of time might you offer as a prepay for your customers at the time of purchase?

- Aside from the time of initial sale, when during your customer lifecycle might you offer a prepay?

Are you getting some good ideas on how to increase the Amount of each Transaction?

Remember, you don't have to implement all - or even most - of these ideas in your business. In fact, some of these may not even apply to your business model! Our Strategy Index by Niche at the end of the book can help you narrow down your options, if you need.

The idea is to pick one, implement it, test for a result you like, and then repeat. Implementation and results are incremental!

Which brings us to our next chapter, on the last of the three variables in our equation: Increasing the Quantity of Customers.

Increasing the Quantity of Customers

"The purpose of business is to create and keep a customer." - Peter Drucker

The last variable in our FAQ equation is Q for the Quantity of Customers that do business with you.

Most business growth books and courses are around *solely* this topic - increasing the quantity of customers, i.e. how to get more leads, more sales, etc.

This all comes down to - in funnel parlance - filling the Top of the Funnel, also known as your "ToFu".

The top of your funnel includes all the steps *before* someone becomes a customer of yours.

For example, it includes seeing your ad (Impression), clicking on your ad, reading your landing page, opting in, then purchasing.

So how do we increase the number of customers that come out the end of *your* funnel?

The following strategies are going to do this in one of a few ways.

Some are going to take your *existing* funnel and patch the leaky holes where prospects are falling out instead of buying.

Other strategies are going to widen parts of your existing funnel so there's higher throughput of prospects becoming customers.

And many strategies are going to remind you of the other ways you can be *filling* your funnel that you might not be doing in your business.

With that said, let's get into a favorite strategy of mine that doesn't change your advertising, or how you fill your funnel; it simply leverages what you're *already* doing and captures some of the sales you're missing.

Downsells

Not every prospect is going to buy your main product or service from you. And that's okay. Before they decide *not* to buy, though, how else might you be able to serve their needs?

When a prospect says no to your main offer and you have a lower priced offer to still get a sale, you have what's called a Downsell.

See, the chasm between a prospect spending zero with you and spending even one penny is gigantic. Once they've spent even a tiny bit with you, they're no longer a prospect and are instead now a customer.

Once they are a customer, they can spend *more* with you as you expand your F and A, in the ways we covered in the previous sections.

Remember the story about the Financial Times from the last chapter? For customers who decide not to subscribe to their print edition, guess what the natural downsell is? Their cheaper online edition!

Remember, a downsell is all about offering a slightly less expensive or scaled-back version of your product or service when a customer hesitates about the initial offer. It's a fantastic way to salvage a potential sale and keep customers happy.

And that's all without *discounting* your main offer.

Imagine a customer is browsing your online store and adds a high-end, annual software license to their cart. They get to the checkout, and bam, sticker shock!

Instead of letting them abandon the purchase, swoop in with an easy downsell. Offer them a *monthly* subscription instead.

It's a smaller commitment, less intimidating on the wallet, and you still gain a loyal customer. You can even sweeten the deal with a "cancel anytime" option or money back guarantee for added peace of mind.

Or consider Amazon Prime. They've mastered the art of the downsell. When someone signs up for a free trial but doesn't convert to a paid membership right away, Amazon doesn't just give up. Instead, they offer a downsell: an extra month of Prime benefits at no cost. It's a brilliant way to hook users, get them addicted to the sweet perks of Prime membership, and increase their chances of converting to a paid membership.

Note that this doesn't detract from the prospective subscribers on a free trial who *do* convert to paid members. It's only offered as a downsell to those who choose *not* to convert.

Let's say you're selling online courses. A prospect is eyeing your premium package, which includes tons of bonus material and personalized coaching. They love the idea but hesitate at the price.

Here's your downsell moment! Offer them a standard package that still delivers core value but at a more accessible price point. Maybe it has fewer bonus features or group coaching instead of one-on-one.

The idea with a downsell is that you're meeting their needs while still generating revenue.

Remember, the key is to present your downsell as a valuable alternative, not a consolation prize. Highlight the benefits, address their concerns, and make it irresistible. You'll be amazed at how many "almost lost" customers you can convert into happy buyers.

Put it into Action!

- What kind of downsell offer could you add into your funnel for those that decline your primary offer?

- What might a trimmed down, lower cost version of your core offer look like?

- Where in your sales funnel and follow up sequences will you offer this downsell?

Expand Up Your Supply Chain

One of the strategies shared in Scaling Up that I love - and even more so love to help implement - is strategy that makes sense for businesses with a supply chain, or a high cost of goods sold (CoGS).

As you look at your expense categories, what are the biggest expenses that you have?

Which - if any - of those expenses can you bring in house, either in the form of a new division, an acquisition, or an entirely new business?

I had the pleasure of visiting Ari Weinzweig and his team at Zingerman's in Ann Arbor, and their story is one I love to share.

Zingerman's started in 1982 when Paul Saginaw and Ari Weinzweig opened a small deli in the college town of Ann Arbor, Michigan. They had a simple goal: to make the best sandwiches in the world.

Zingerman's quickly became known for its delicious sandwiches, made with high-quality ingredients and served on house-baked bread.

As Ari and his team looked at their expenses, they realized that in running their deli, one of their biggest expenses was... the bread for their sandwiches.

So in 1988, they opened Zingerman's Bakehouse to supply their deli with fresh bread. The bakehouse's first customer was of course the deli. And then came the additional wholesale clients like restaurants and grocery stores. Soon, though, it, too, became a destination in its own right, and today it is one of the most respected bakeries in the country.

Then, in the 1990s, Zingerman's repeated the process and saw that their next biggest expenses were dairy followed by coffee.

As a deli they needed cheese for their sandwiches, milk for their coffee, cream cheese for their bagels, and so on.

So in 1992 they launched Zingerman's Creamery and a few years later, in 1999, Zingerman's Coffee Company. Visiting their coffee company was an especially special treat for me, a lover of coffee, as it wasn't just a café. They had expanded beyond just *serving* coffee to consumers, and beyond wholesaling of roasted coffee beans, and beyond just *roasting* imported coffees, but to be a coffee importer, too!

These are typically four *different* businesses! At Zingerman's, though, they had worked their way up their supply chain once again, and rolled all the parts of the coffee business into one.

These businesses all share the same commitment to quality and customer service that has made Zingerman's a success.

Today, Zingerman's is a thriving community of food businesses that includes the original deli, the bakehouse, the creamery, the coffee company, and a variety of other food-related businesses.

What's great about their story is that they worked their way through their biggest expenses, launching new businesses to serve themselves as a customer, they also expanded to serve the community at large.

Each of their new businesses brought in new wholesale and direct consumer customers.

From selling their bread, dairy, and coffee to other restaurants, to serving coffee to customers in their café, each business not only reduced expenses and increased profits, it also expanded them into new markets.

One of my clients, in looking at his expenses, saw a large expense category in acquiring raw ingredients from farms directly. That observation turned into visiting some of the farms which started the conversations around *acquiring* some of the farms.

Working your way up your supply chain not only can help you to reduce your expenses, it can help you to safeguard your supply chain, make money from your "competitors" and expand your Quantity of Customers.

Put it into Action!

- As you look at your financials, where are you spending an outsized portion of your expenses?

- What opportunities are there for you to bring an expense category in house - or launch a new business - and expand your market with that new service?

- How could bringing that part of your supply chain in house impact your profitability, safeguard your operations, or increase your Quantity of Customers?

Filling Your Top of Funnel

Implementing everything you've learned so far will all help you to do more with the customers you already have, but what about getting more customers into your Top of Funnel (ToFu)?

Each of the strategies in the rest of this chapter has had dozens of entire books written on them, so this is by no means meant to be a comprehensive deep dive into each topic.

Instead, think of the following strategies as "conversation starters" to get you asking if you are already using each strategy, *could* be using each strategy, or could be doing each *better*.

With that disclaimer out of the way, and the intention set, let's dive in.

As a "dot connector" - finding the unseen patterns - one of my favorite tactics is to help transplant an idea that's working for one business owner and make it work in *another* business.

This is what I call "cross pollination of ideas" and it's beautiful to see it happen.

For example, one of my clients had a brick and mortar retail store and - like many business owners - was feeling stuck in her business. She wasn't seeing the growth she wanted with the strategies she'd been using.

She was seeing success, and was profitable, but the growth just wasn't where she wanted it to be.

Sitting across the table from her at one of our Mastermind meetings was an e-commerce store owner who - like her - was seeing success in his business but was also tapping out his existing sales channels.

Simply by cross pollinating sales channels between the two businesses, both businesses were able to leverage the best practices of the other business, add a new sales channel, and get more sales!

See, the retail store owner had successfully been using direct mail to bring new customers into the shop. Direct mail isn't a strategy often used by newer e-commerce businesses, but it's worked for decades...

Which brings us to our first strategy, Direct Mail!

Direct Mail

Many businesses these days don't use direct mail when it's still quite effective at bringing in new customers who've never heard of you.

To successfully implement direct mail to bring in *new* customers, you're going to need a few things.

Your Direct Mail List

For starters, you're going to need a list - a list of prospective customers to mail.

But where do you find a list? You can buy lists online pretty easily, but I've always worked with a list broker or lead generation specialist to create lists.

The real challenge is dialing in exactly *who* you want on your list. And that's the beauty of direct mail versus, say, a billboard, or TV ad. With direct mail, you can choose exactly what household gets your message - and who doesn't.

If you already have an established customer list, you can get your list profiled by a third party vendor to identify not just the demographic qualities of your customers, but also their psychographic profiles. With this in hand, you can then go to your list broker and get more leads like your ideal customers.

A good list analysis will even break down who your best - and worst -

customers are categorically.

Whenever I do this list analysis for a project, we find that there are some segments *overrepresented* in the prospect list that we are clearly attracting - but they don't buy, or they buy very little. We can then work to more actively *repel* these categories in our copy and list purchasing.

Conversely, we typically find that there are a handful of segments (or "clusters") that spend really well - but are *underrepresented* on our prospect list. We're doing a poor job attracting those prospects, but when they *do* buy, they're very high value customers.

We then work to do a better job attracting those ideal buyers in our copy, offers, and lists.

And then we find the sweet spot of the segments that we attract well who spend well; we just want more of them. This is *perfect* for your list broker to work with.

For our current list of favorite resources for list profiling, list brokering, and direct mail, visit the Bonuses section of *YourBusinessGrowthPlaybook.com*

Your Direct Mail Offer

Next up, you'll need to figure out what exactly it is that you're going to be offering in your direct mail campaign.

Remember, these are typically suspects who've never heard of you and your goal is to get them to - for starters not throw your direct mail pieces into the garbage - indicate interest.

This isn't where you go for a high end sale. This is where you create your irresistible offer that gets them to opt-in - just like an online campaign.

You might have a free gift offer, a free plus shipping and handling offer, a buy one get one free offer, etc. You can even lose money on this first sale. You just want to get someone to go from getting a mail piece to indicating interest so you can then send your follow up marketing to a much higher quality prospect.

Your Direct Mail Piece(s)

Now that you have a list and an offer, you'll need to actually figure out what you're going to be mailing.

This can range from a simple postcard, to a letter, to a FedEx envelope, or if you're like my friend Jon, a watermelon!

One day, years ago, I swung past the post office to pick up mail for one of my businesses; I also had a note from the post office that a package was waiting for me.

I brought the slip over to the counter to see what treasures awaited, and they went looking around for a bit. When the clerk returned, she was carrying a giant inflatable playground ball from my friend Ted.

Taped onto it was a letter for me.

It certainly got my attention, I had a laugh, but when I went to get rid of the ball, it wouldn't even fit in the trash can outside the post office. It was too big!

I had to take the darn thing home and find a way to get rid of it!

Ted made sure that everyone he mailed picked up, handled, and interacted with his direct mail pieces.

Jon famously did the same thing, but by attaching his letter to watermelons and shipping those. Yes, the post office - with the right postage - will deliver an unboxed watermelon!

Now you don't have to be that creative - though it works. You can instead start with something simple and go from there.

Especially with a brand new list, you don't know how many of the leads have invalid addresses - though you can scrub the list ahead of time - so starting with a simple large postcard is a good way to validate your list.

When you get the returned mail back for invalid addresses, you can remove those, and then spend more on your follow up mailings to the valid addresses.

If you have a higher end offer and you've mastered increasing your F and A - then you can outspend your competition.

You can send a FedEx mailer, a Tyvek envelope, or even a physical box to your prospects. It'll cost a bit more to mail, but if your CLV is high enough, you know your piece will get past the gatekeepers and into your prospects hands.

Put it into Action!

- With these ideas, how can you start implementing direct mail to bring in new leads for your business?

- How well have you defined your ideal customer? Where are you going to get a list of prospects who match your profile?

- What will you send them?

Search Engine Optimization (SEO)

Now for prospects searching online - either for answers to questions your prospects have, or more specifically for the solution you have to offer - you want to show up high on their search results.

Optimizing your site for search engines is called Search Engine Optimization (or "SEO" for short) and it's not something that just happens automatically.

There are a number of tactics you need to apply to your website - and any new content you put online - to help it rank well and show up to your ideal prospects.

Google and the rest of the search engines are pretty good at figuring out what your website content is about, but... the more you help, the more in control you are of *how* your website shows up in search results.

At the very least, having well-chosen page titles and descriptions will help.

Using free tools like Yoast or Rank Math for all of your on-page SEO will help you quickly optimize individual pages for the keywords you're looking to own.

What's amazing if you look at the difference in traffic between top positions on search engines is that, typically, for each spot you drop, you lose about *half* the traffic.

That means the website in first position gets about double the traffic as the site in the number two spot.

And the second site gets about double the traffic as the third result.

So by the time you're off the first page, or even near the bottom, you're getting a tiny *fraction* of the potential traffic.

Moving up even just one position for some of your ideal keywords is huge. Getting into those coveted first few positions is game changing.

If you don't have an active SEO strategy in place, get one of the free SEO plugins, and start by making sure that all *new* content you publish is positioned well for SEO.

Concurrently, get an SEO audit (with an agency or a free/paid tool online) for your existing content and start optimizing your *existing* content.

The time needed to do this will depend on the size of your site and how many pages you have. You can do this on your own, or you can find an agency or freelancer to help you just "get it done."

Thirdly, consider strategically - and with the help of tools - what pages you want to publish to help you rank better - or at all - for the keywords and phrases you want traffic for.

Lastly, and this is often one of the most challenging and time consuming parts, you'll want to start building up your backlinks from real/legit sites to specific pages on your site.

Avoid hacky spam links or "link building" services as they typically cause more harm than good, and don't serve you well in the long run.

One of our clients had been doing zero SEO but, amazingly, was ranking pretty well for a few highly targeted keywords. One of the best keywords he was ranking for was actually a page with *no* content, but it just had the right headline and page title!

This was such low hanging fruit to optimize, by adding the right content, and starting to actually deliver on the content readers were looking for. Your website probably also has low hanging fruits like these that you can quickly optimize and improve your rankings.

Local SEO

If you have a local business or you serve specific geographic markets, there is a subset of SEO you'll want to dial in immediately, and that's local SEO.

The more search engines understand how you serve a very local market, the better, and that often comes from flagging this to them in various directories and internal listings with your geographic service areas and address.

Just how big of a deal is this for local businesses?

Google found that 78% of people who search on their phone for a nearby service or solution visit the business *within one day*!

Furthermore, they found that 28% of local searches end up in a purchase.

One of the key components of local SEO is the optimization of Google My Business (GMB) listings. By creating and maintaining an accurate and detailed GMB profile, your business can appear correctly in local search results and Google Maps.

This includes providing essential information such as the business name, address, phone number, hours of operation, and categories. Encouraging customer reviews and responding to them can also improve your business's credibility and visibility in local searches.

Apple's equivalent of GMB for Apple Maps is called Apple Business Connect. ABC allows you to create and manage your presence on Apple Maps which also helps when customers are using Siri or other Apple products.

With Apple Business Connect, you can claim your business listing, update your information such as business name, address, phone number, hours of operation, and website. You can also add photos, special offers, and other relevant details to improve your visibility and attract local customers. And, like GMB, this is where you manage customer reviews and respond to inquiries.

In addition to GMB and ABC, local SEO involves optimizing your website itself for local keywords, which often include geographic terms.

This can be achieved through on-page SEO techniques, such as incorporating location-based keywords in titles, meta descriptions, and content.

Building local citations - mentions of your business on other websites, directories, and social media platforms - also plays a big role in establishing authority and relevance in local search results.

Specifically, you want your business name, physical address, phone number, and website listed in the right directories. Together these are often referred to as your "NAP" (or "NAPW"). There are dozens of directories you want to be in for this purpose and many services that will submit you to - and maintain your listings - in these directories for you.

SEO tools change often. For the latest tools and resources we like, visit YourBusinessGrowthPlaybook.com and click Bonuses.

Quick SEO Fixes

The first thing we do when helping a client figure out how they're doing with SEO and what the opportunities are is making sure analytics tools are set up correctly.

These are free, and come from search engine providers like Google. At a minimum, you want to have your Google Analytics in place, along with your Google Search Console (GSC) setup and configured.

With the tooling and tracking in place, we can then start looking at how well a site is performing and ranking, what it's ranking well for, what it's ranking okay for, and where the opportunities are.

GSC is a free web service provided by Google that helps you monitor, maintain, and optimize your website's presence in Google search results. As a business owner, using GSC can provide you with the quick and actionable items needed to improve your website's performance in search engines.

Importantly, you'll now be able to track clicks, impressions, and rankings for your website to understand traffic sources.

You'll also be able to see what issues both desktop and mobile users are facing on your site so you can improve their experience - which improves your rankings.

Lastly, you'll learn your Core Web Vitals so you can improve loading performance for your website visitors.

This gives us a baseline from which to improve.

Sometimes a few tweaks to your website - or adding on a few free tools and services - is all it takes to bring your website grade from a D to an A.

Next up, we use free On Page SEO tools to see how well optimized each page on the site is, starting with the most important pages for lead generation and traffic.

Fixing up individual pages - as well as the site overall - starts to then make a difference in how well a business ranks and we can then measure *quantitatively* the improvement.

Then we can bring in the powerful paid tools to really ramp up the rankings on not just existing site content - but to plan for and create *new* content going forward.

This brings us to content marketing.

Put it into Action!

- What specific keywords or phrases will you target to attract your ideal problem (or solution) aware prospect to your website?

- How do you plan to monitor your keywords, traffic, and rankings?

- Beyond just traffic, what metrics will you use to measure the quality of the leads from your SEO?

Content Marketing

Content marketing and SEO go hand in hand, but content marketing is all around creating original content that attracts your ideal prospect.

For prospects that are solution aware, they'll find you by searching for your company name, or the name of the product or service you have to offer.

But for prospects that may not even be problem aware yet... you have your content. You're getting in front of them before they even *know* what the solution is or that you're the solution.

So, ask yourself:

What questions are your prospects asking?

What problems do they face that they are going online to solve?

What are the water cooler conversations that your prospects have?

Who are your ideal prospects – the ones who don't know they have a problem yet - searching for online?

These are all great starting points for content on your website. Search engines love to see websites that are posting recent and *original* content. And it's a good indication to your website visitors that you're a legit and active business, too!

This original content is also a great jumping off point for your social media, but more on that later in the chapter!

Put it into Action!

- What are a dozen or two questions that your ideal customers ask?

- How will you promote your new content beyond just publishing it on your website?

- What clear Calls to Action (CTAs) will you include in your content?

Pay Per Click (PCC) Advertising

One of the most familiar levers you will know about for increasing the quantity of customers if you do any kind of business online is Pay Per Click ("PPC") advertising. Think Google AdWords, Bing Ads, Facebook Ads, etc.

But the concept is much broader than just the big well known platforms. PPC, at its heart, means that, instead of paying for an *impression* of your ad, you're only paying when someone *clicks* on your ad. Hence the pay per *click*.

PPC advertising sits between higher in the funnel PPM advertising and lower in the funnel CPA or PPL ads.

How does PPC differ?

Pay Per Impression (PPM) advertising where you pay for how many times the ad is *shown*.

Cost Per Action (CPA) is when you pay for users taking an *action* like downloading your app, attending a webinar, signing up for your newsletter, are making a purchase.

Pay Per Lead (PPL) is when you pay for a lead, i.e. an opt-in.

The higher up in the funnel it is, the less valuable an action is to you (i.e. an impression) and the further down the funnel you go, the *more* valuable it is (i.e. a purchase).

Depending on what you're selling, there are often very niche places you can run PPC ads, too. For example, if you're selling your book, you'd obviously use Amazon's PPC platform. If you run a restaurant, you might use Yelp's PPC platform.

The good thing about PPC is that once you dial it in, you can generally scale it up - to a limit.

For a data business I was running, we got started early in PPC. We found that when we spent a dollar, we could generally get $2-4 back in return right away. So our Return on Ad Spend (or "RoAS") was 200-400%. Which is great!

So we scaled up from $10k/month to $20k/month in ad spend. Our RoAS dropped, but we were still quite profitable. It was somewhere in the 150-250% range. So we scaled up again to $30k/month and while the RoAS dropped again, it was still profitable. At around $40k/mo we were breaking even on the front end. But... this was for a subscription-based business, which meant when we looked at that Customer Lifetime Value... It was great!

Unfortunately... we made one mistake we never made again. We took our eye off our PPC reporting. We let the campaign keep running on autopilot, bringing in new customers while we worked on other parts of the business.

The next thing we knew, without anything changing, we were suddenly only seeing around 50% RoAS. That meant for every dollar we spent on ads... we were only getting $0.50 back!

And it continued to get worse.

It was around that time we brought in an agency to manage our PPC for us. Almost overnight, through some rather simple strategies, they were able to cut our ad spend in half AND double the results, so that was a 4x improvement.

That was only possible because someone else was now tasked with overseeing and optimizing the account on a daily basis.

So the takeaway for you here is that PPC *can* deliver great results. But you can't just let it run on autopilot.

Alphabet (Google) generates over 75% of its revenue from AdWords. That's billions of dollars (like ~$175 billion in 2023). That's only possible because it works for businesses large and small, from Fortune 100 down to mom and pop shops.

Your competitors are using PPC. You may even have tried it. And it can work for you, too.

But... you need a congruent funnel from the ad headline to ad copy to the landing page to the offer and so on. And you need someone - either you, a team member, a freelancer, or an agency - actively managing and optimizing the account for you.

Put it into Action!

- What PPC campaigns could you be running for your business to bring in prospects who are problem or solution aware?

- What specific keywords or audience segments will you target?

- Who is going to create and manage your PPC campaigns for you?

Affiliates / Partners

Like many of our strategies that work across business models and business types, one of my favorites has been in use for thousands of years - literally.

Way back in 55 BC, Julius Caesar had a problem many business owners still face today. He needed more people to get into his funnel.

In your case, you want more customers. In his case, he needed more soldiers for the Roman army.

So what did Caesar do? He promised 300 *sestertii* to any soldier who referred another soldier to join his army. As a frame of reference, at the time, common legionary soldiers made about 900 *sestertii* a year in salary, so this was a *huge* referral fee.

While that may have been the first documented usage of paying out referral fees, it's a strategy used across industries even today.

Amazon Associates, for example, pays out *billions* of dollars a year to its "associates" who refer them new business. ClickBank, another huge marketplace for referrals, has also paid out billions of dollars to referral partners.

And this is the exact strategy that I've used, too. Both in my own businesses and with clients' businesses again and again.

One of the ways that I've launched and built businesses is through affiliate partners. These are people with lists of your ideal customer that are willing to promote what you are selling to their list.

While there are many marketplaces online where you can list your products and people can find your offer and send it to their list, most all successful affiliate partner relationships typically come from individual relationships.

Depending on the size of your business, it may be you as the business owner tapping into your existing network and developing new relationships with affiliates, or you may have a dedicated person on your team responsible for managing your affiliates (an Affiliate Manager).

Either way, relationship management is the key here.

For a good affiliate partnership to work, you want to make sure you have your product and offer dialed in and that you know how to sell it. You want a well converting funnel that your affiliates can then help fill.

That last point bears repeating: do *not* send affiliate traffic into unproven funnels. You need to *know* you have a well converting offer and funnel before making it available to affiliates!

You also want to make it as easy as possible for your affiliate partners to promote you. This means creating "done for you" marketing, graphics, media, and "swipe" copy that they can use.

The more work you do to help your partner be successful, the easier it will be for them to promote your offer.

One thing we've seen when working with affiliates is that list *quality* matters a lot in terms of setting expectations.

We had one affiliate with an email list of over 200,000 - but with single digit opens and no clicks. So the list *quality* was complete garbage.

Conversely, we had an affiliate with a teeny list of merely 600 - but these were 600 high end *customers*. All of them were *buyers* and followed his lead. His email open rates and click through rates were astronomical. So when he suggested they join him on a webinar, they did. And when he said why they should buy from us, they did.

So be mindful of list size, but realize that *quality* is more important! I've found asking questions like "how many people do you typically get onto a webinar?" or "how have your past few promotions to your list performed?" help to dial in realistic expectations.

In terms of the mechanics, you're typically going to offer a revenue share to your affiliates. This can be anywhere from 10-60% of gross revenue.

The higher the profit margin and lower the cost of goods, the higher the affiliate payout is, i.e. for software and online courses. The lower the profit margin and higher the cost of goods, the lower the payout is, i.e. for physical goods.

In some rare cases, when you have your funnel really dialed in and you know what your customers are really worth, you can even offer 100% of the gross revenue on *the initial transaction* to your affiliates.

Again, if you know your numbers really well, it can even be a flat rate per lead, but percentage of sales is far more common.

Then, you just need to make sure your CRM or affiliate platform provides you with unique links to give to your affiliate partners so you know where any leads or customers they send you come from.

Depending on the size of your business and the size of your affiliate partners' business, they may look for a "swap" where they run your affiliate promotion to their list, but - because you have the same ideal customer - you also run a promotion for them to your list.

Put it into Action!

- Who else has customers like your ideal customer?

- What "done for you" marketing could you offer to prospective affiliates to send you traffic, leads, and customers?

- Who can you call, like today, and recruit to be an affiliate partner of yours?

Cold Outbound Emailing

Before we get into cold outbound email marketing, be mindful that regulations regarding this are likely changing. We don't get into fax marketing because that's no longer a thing due to laws.

And while unsolicited email to consumers is almost guaranteed to be considered spam and in violation of some laws, direct email to businesses is often viewed differently. Again, be compliant, and don't go breaking any laws on this - or anything you're doing!

If you look at any B2B business that's grown, it's very often due to cold outbound emailing.

This - like direct mail - comes down to getting a list of businesses, specifically with the decision maker's email address, and sending an email campaign to them.

The goal of your outbound campaign is again to get someone to "raise their hand" and indicate interest. This is almost always in the form of them replying back expressing interest or asking to schedule a call with you.

There are many platforms that you can use for your cold B2B outreach, and many of these even have lead generation built in so you can create your own list right in the tool and then begin your outreach.

Some of these tools will even create your outbound email campaigns for you!

As these tools are constantly evolving, you can see the latest ones we're liking on our free book resource page at

---

Put it into Action!

- Who could you be emailing about doing business with you? Who is your ideal customer?

- What will you write in your email to resonate with your ideal customer and elicit genuine interest?

- What would your Call to Action be in the email? To reply back? Schedule a call? Something else?

Cold Calling / Telemarketing

Like faxing of decades past, and emailing of years ago, the rules around cold calling have changed, too. This strategy is much more commonly used for B2B businesses, and the laws and regulations around this tactic may change in the future.

In the interim, if you're selling to businesses, a common strategy is simply to pick up the phone and call them.

A colleague of mine years ago was a real estate agent and every morning started his day with 300 outbound cold calls to homeowners. As you can imagine, most of the calls went unanswered, ended up in voicemail, annoyed the homeowner, or got someone who wasn't interested.

He was fine with all of those "Nos" because he didn't need that many "Yesses." From all of his morning calls, he'd get a few listing appointments, where you go out and meet with the homeowner and pitch them on listing their home with you. Some of those turned into listings and some of those listings turned into sold homes.

He did this every single morning. 300 calls in the morning. Then listing appointments. Then closings.

And boy did he have closings!

Whereas the typical Realtor at the time sold 0.6 properties a *year*, he was closing 30 homes a *month*.

Not from billboards, our TV advertising, or referrals, or any other source. All simply from making his calls like clockwork every single morning.

One of my B2B clients scaled his business beautifully by simply picking up the phone and "dialing for dollars" every morning.

His goal from a cold outbound call was to get someone on the phone and set an appointment for a one on one sales call. Then, during that sales call, he'd close them on an engagement.

At first, he was making a few hundred calls a week, mostly in the mornings, and then spent the rest of his time in the sales meetings and doing actual client work that he had closed.

It got to the point, though, where it made sense to bring someone on to help out with these sales. The natural next hire is to bring on a Sales Development Rep - or SDR - to make these outbound sales and set appointments for you.

Now with someone making outbound calls full-time, he went from a few hundred outbound calls a week to 1,500. And instead of making *any* of the calls on his own, he went to making *none* and instead used that newfound time to show up to all the sales meetings that his SDR was putting on his calendar for him.

This is now very scalable. Because all you do is add another SDR and you double the number of sales meetings you have.

Don't expect SDRs to be as effective as you are at outbound calls. They don't have to be. They can be less effective as they are *scalable*. Their job is to qualify suspects and put sales calls on your calendar.

Pretty soon you can have sales reps handling those sales calls, too, and now you have a scaling business that can turn on the Top of Funnel faucet!

Put it into Action!

- If you're selling to businesses, where can you get a list of businesses you want to qualify into a sales meeting?

- What can you say to them when they *do* answer the phone to qualify them and then help them schedule a sales call?

- How will you consistently track and manage your calls to measure the success of your campaign?

Social Media

Social Media is an ever-changing space with new platforms launching and old ones dying out. The MySpace and Friendster of yesterday go away and the Instagrams and TikToks of the world emerge. Even this sentence will be dated as you read this!

Nuances between platforms aside, the general *strategies* between them are the same. And all of it comes down to Community, Content, Engagement, and Calls to Action (CTAs).

And while yes, on some platforms you can't post links, and others are purely video, and others only allow short form text, and some day they'll be only VR or smellovision or something we can't even yet imagine, you still need a *community*.

Your Community are your followers, your subscribers, your hashtag followers, your public groups, your private group members, and so on.

These are the humans who see the Content that you post.

Posting content that nobody sees, won't get you any Engagement.

Posting Content that your Community sees but doesn't care about, *also* won't get you any Engagement.

Posting Content that your Community sees and cares about may get Engagement, but if it doesn't have any Calls to Action, won't get any *results*.

So let's start with Community.

Building a community is all about creating a space where your target audience feels like they belong and that you're speaking directly to them. Think of it like inviting them into your living room for a chat.

Respond to comments, ask for their opinions, and share their stories. When people feel valued, they're more likely to stick around and even spread the word about your business.

Now, let's talk about content. This is your chance to show off what you're all about. Share content and posts that are not just promotional but also fun, informative, or entertaining. Mix it up with videos, behind-the-scenes glimpses, or even a funny meme that relates to your brand.

Storytelling is a powerful tool here - people love to hear about your journey, your challenges, and your wins. When your content resonates with them, they're more likely to engage and share it with their own friends.

This brings us to Engagement - where the real connection happens. The easy approach is to just "post and ghost", but you want to do far more. Dive into the comments, ask questions, and encourage discussions.

For example, you could run a poll to see what your audience thinks about a new product or ask for their favorite tips related to your products, services, or even industry. The more you interact, the more your audience will feel like they're part of something special. Plus, it gives you valuable insights into what they really care about.

Finally, for your clear Call to Action (CTA), make sure you guide your audience on what to do next. Whether it's "Check out our latest collection!" or "Sign up for our newsletter for exclusive deals!" make sure your CTAs are clear, friendly, inviting, and easy.

Like any CTA in any other marketing channel, use language that creates a sense of urgency. When your audience knows exactly what you want them to do, they're more likely to take that step.

But social media shouldn't be where your *entire* business is based. That's where it starts to get risky.

Your Community - Someone Else's Rules

As you build your community out on the various social media platforms of your choosing, be mindful that a simple change in laws, rules, policies, and fad can take your highly performing account and... turn it into nothing overnight or over months.

You *never* want to be single-platform and "all in" in one place. The sooner you can connect with your Community *outside* of one social media platform the better. That means helping them to opt-in and give you permission to follow up in other ways, i.e. phone, email, text, snail mail, and so on.

Too many businesses have built everything on one platform only to see the algorithm destroy their business overnight.

For example, BuzzFeed, Vice, and the Huffington Post all used to get a majority of their traffic and readership from Facebook. This led to multi-billion dollar valuations for all three of their businesses.

When Facebook changed their algorithm and what it showed in "the feed", traffic to these sites nearly dried up overnight. What had been working suddenly stopped working.

This tanked the valuations of their businesses by billions of dollars.

This has famously happened across other platforms like YouTube and

Instagram, too. Businesses (content creators) with huge followings found themselves suddenly in violation of a platform rule and had their accounts suspended or shutdown. This even happens when they are *not* in violation of any rule, but a user *reports* that they are.

Don't get me wrong, when you have a lead source, and it's producing for you, that's a *good* thing. You just don't want to build your entire business on one lead source *especially* if you don't own the list with a way to reach your audience *outside* of that platform.

Savvy businesses move their followers into their funnels as soon and as often as possible.

Beyond Just Posts

Leveraging social media can also be about far more than just your posts. Many platforms let you create your own private groups or communities where you can engage with your audience on a deeper - and more private - level.

The social media platform provides the leads who want to apply for (read: qualify) or pay to join your group.

The members/subscribers in your groups are then either qualified prospects or entry level buyers that you can then engage 1:1 and bring deeper into your funnel.

There are entire books and programs that dive deeper into this strategy, but my goal here is to expand your perspective on how social media can be used for more than just content posts - but for entire lead generation funnels with private groups.

Put it into Action!

- On which platforms is your business most active? What other platforms should you consider?

- How well does your content resonate with your community? How could you increase engagement?

- How effectively are you moving your engaged community off of the platform and onto your own list?

Media / Press / PR

While most of your advertising strategies involve you talking about your business (except for referrals and affiliate partners), earned media, press and PR are about third parties putting you in front of their audiences and telling a story where you're the hero.

Imagine your ideal customer turning on their TV in the morning, opening their news app, or listening to the radio on their commute to work and hearing a story about *you* from the same credible news sources they know, like, and trust.

You've just cut through all the clutter, and had your message delivered to your ideal customer on a silver platter in the way that they're most receptive to.

That's what earned media is all about.

Yes, you can put out press releases that you or your PR person write up and put out on "the wire", but those rarely get picked up. You'll get some good play on sites that choose to publish your release. But those are still your own words about you.

Where the real magic happens is when individual publications pick up on your story and write their *own* story about you.

This, however, very often comes down to individually pitching journalists, developing stories for and *with* them, and having real human relationships with the writers who put stories out in their publications.

For one of our businesses, we got out ahead of the curve of a trend coming in the marketplace. We established ourselves as the experts in the space with the real data to show what was going on in the market.

From this data, we crafted informative press releases about what was happening with trends, data points of note, and real data.

This, in turn, was valuable to publications. As a result, for a few years, it seemed not a day went by that print, online, TV, and radio weren't interviewing us.

And when we were in the news... we could see the spike in website visitors, opt-ins, and new customers. Like clockwork.

Now, it's unrealistic to expect that a press release centered on you and your business is going to get any traction or result in a steady flow of new business. A good story, however, in front of your target audience, may get you a spike in new visibility or new business, but it's generally short lived.

To get started, at a minimum have a press kit or a press page on your website. This should include the info that the press will need to know about you and your business, your contact info, as well as some high-res photos of you and your business that they can use in their stories, if they like.

The next thing - and this is the hardest, yet most important part - is to have your PR person (which might be you) draft up compelling story ideas to pitch to the journalists you've been developing relationships with.

The more your stories relate to what's currently happening in the market, community, and world, the better of an angle you'll have with the journalists. Remember, they have deadlines and stories they have to publish. The more you're helping them do their job, the better.

Lastly, there are a number of platforms that connect experts like you with journalists so that when they're writing a story, they can get industry and expert quotes.

You can get a current list of these kinds of platforms under Bonuses at *YourBusinessGrowthPlaybook.com*

Put it into Action!

- Do you have your press kit ready?

- How about a press or media page on your website?

- What relevant stories can you pitch to the media that would help them and their readers?

Traditional Advertising

Traditional advertising encompasses the classic methods of promoting your business that have stood the test of time since before you and I were born.

This includes print ads in newspapers and magazines, commercials on television and radio, billboards along busy roads, and even those colorful flyers that show up in your mailbox. These methods can be incredibly effective in helping you reach your target audience and grow your business.

Unlike many of our more "targeted" strategies above, the biggest advantages of traditional advertising is its broad reach.

When you choose the right media channels, you can connect with a large number of people. For local businesses, advertising in community newspapers or on local radio stations can be particularly beneficial, as it allows you to attract customers right in your area. The visibility you gain from these ads can significantly increase foot traffic and inquiries.

While typically reserved for much bigger businesses, branding *does* matter, and building brand awareness is another benefit of traditional advertising. When potential customers see your brand in print or on TV, it creates a lasting impression. The more frequently they encounter your ad, name, logo, or jingle, the more likely they are to think of you when they need your products or services. This consistent exposure helps establish your business as a recognizable and trusted option in the marketplace.

Moreover, traditional advertising allows for geographically targeted messaging. You can tailor your ads to specific demographics based on the media you choose. For instance, if you know your ideal customers read a particular magazine or listen to a specific radio station, placing your ads there can effectively reach the right audience, which... can lead to higher engagement and conversion rates.

Many consumers also perceive traditional advertising as more credible than digital ads. A well-placed ad in a reputable publication or a catchy commercial on a popular TV channel can help your business establish trust, credibility, and legitimacy. This credibility can be crucial in building trust with potential customers, especially if they are unfamiliar with your brand.

Lastly, traditional advertising can foster local engagement. By sponsoring community events or running promotions that resonate with your audience, you can create a buzz around your business. This not only helps you connect with your community but also encourages word-of-mouth referrals, which can be incredibly powerful. Which... is what we'll be getting to in the next section!

To make traditional advertising work for you, you have to really know your target audience, which we dive into deeply in Your Action Plan. Think about who your ideal customers are, what they like, and where they hang out. This will help you pick the right places to advertise, whether it's local newspapers, radio stations, or specific magazines. Your message should be clear and engaging with a strong call to action to get potential customers to take the next step.

There is almost no limit to how much you *can* spend on traditional advertising, so set a budget that fits your overall marketing plan, and keep an eye on how much different advertising methods cost.

While a little more challenging than with digital ads, you'll want to - as best you can - track how well your ads are doing. Using unique phone numbers, promo codes, or simply asking customers how they found you can give you great insights into what's working best for your business.

One business we were working with was putting together ads to go in a traditional magazine. Specifically this was for a magazine tailored for Ultra High Network Individuals, readers with multiple homes, boats, planes, and so forth.

After looking at the rate card of what it cost for a full page ad in this high-end magazine (tens of thousands of dollars), the question came up of what it cost to simply run a plain text classified ad in the back of the magazine. That was only a few *hundred* dollars *and* resulted in a stream of very high quality leads and new business.

Just because you *can* spend a ton on traditional advertising doesn't mean you *should*. There are many great ways - like with the classified ad - that you can see the benefits of traditional advertising without blowing your entire marketing budget.

Put it into Action!

- How could you use more traditional advertising to promote your business?

- What channels make the most sense for your audience? Magazine advertising? TV ads? Radio ads? Newspaper ads?

- What do your ideal customers read, watch, and listen to?

Referrals

For newer local businesses, much of their initial and new business is often word of mouth based referrals. This may come from friends, family, or clients.

Scaling that up, however, can be slow going, especially since most of the new people that can refer you will be from clients. It's a bit of a snowball effect, and it takes time to get that snowball going.

Another great way to encourage that snowball to grow even faster is to generate referrals through referral groups. One of the best known referral groups is Business Networking International also known as BNI.

These groups are specifically focused on members passing each other warm referrals for new business. This differs strongly from *leads* group where members pass each other ice cold leads to cold call. And this is different from a *networking* group where attendees are looking just to meet people and network.

Growing a business by referral can go so well that, for some businesses, they end up shifting their entire business to by referral only. Meaning, they don't have any other sales channels aside from referrals and the referrals provide more than enough business.

Some simple strategies to generate more referrals include simply *asking* your clients for referrals. You can do this at the time of the sale, on delivery, in a follow up, or even all of the above.

You can also include a simple email footer to ask for referrals. Spotlight and highlight your top referrers. Write about them. Thank them. Promote them.

One of my earlier businesses was in the computer service space. Through a business referral group, I was introduced to a woman who upon having coffee with me and learning about my business asked how she could best promote me.

Before I could answer, she asked if she could send out a mail piece to all of her clients about me and my business and tell her clients all about what we had to offer.

I was delighted, and we did indeed send out that mail campaign, and I got new business from it. In fact, I then did the same in kind telling my client base about Sheila's services. This all led to a wonderful referral partner, and in later years a business partner for future ventures.

Now keep in mind with referrals, we're not talking about an affiliate relationship where you're paying someone a portion of the sales to generate leads or sales for you. We cover that more in depth in our chapter on Affiliate Partners.

This is much more personal and warm and typically does not have a financial reward.

So why are your referral partners going to refer you to clients?

Typically it comes down to three big factors.

Your referral partners send you business when they:

- Know you

- Like you

- Trust you

Knowing is easy. People can know who you are from meeting you at networking events, but that doesn't mean they *like* you or even *trust* you yet.

Sometimes liking and trusting come from familiarity.

That can be a matter of prospective referral partners seeing you again and again at local chamber of commerce events, for example, and knowing that you're not fly by night and are around to stay.

But more typically the liking and trusting comes from really getting to know you through one-on-one get togethers, often just over coffee or a meal, or in smaller groups.

Even more powerful is when you connect up with referral partners who serve your same ideal customer.

Can a roofer refer a client to a dentist? Sure. The commonality in their clients is that they are... people. But otherwise, the overlap in needs of someone needing a roof and needing dental work is next to nil.

But is a real estate agent far more able to refer a client to a mortgage broker? Absolutely. They have the exact same ideal customer: someone actively buying real estate.

A SaaS business we were working with added on some great referral partners simply by running live events together with their referral partners. Both companies had platforms that not only served the same market, they complimented each other, too.

When a customer onboarded with one partner, they easily recommended doing business with their counterpart. It was an easy referral and was offered digitally, as well as individually by team members during onboarding.

Many times, if you really dial this in, you'll find the best referral partners are the ones that you empower to do business. In other words, you help their prospects become their customers by becoming *your* customers.

We've seen this happen when working with businesses that help real estate investors invest in properties referring their customers to self directed IRA custodians that then enable those prospects to invest in properties.

This is also common in the real estate example of a real estate agent working with a prospective buyer who isn't prequalified for a loan yet. They refer them to a mortgage broker to get prequalified so that they can then shop for and buy a home.

And another example of this is a retail sports store supporting local events by hosting their event bib pickup in store. The event organizer (think 5k run, marathon, etc) now has a place to set up shop for a day and help their thousands of registrants pickup their bibs and swag bags.

The store suddenly has an influx of traffic, and even a discount for race registrants on the day of their bib pickup. And the event registrants then buy any additional goods they need to make for a successful race, from shoes to shorts to nutrition.

You're reading this book because you're looking to *grow*, so if that sounds like your business, then kudos! You're doing great with referrals.

Now it's time to add on the rest of the channels.

Put it into Action!

- If you are *not* generating business from referrals, how could you start doing that?

- What other industries or professions work with your same ideal customer?

- On the flip side, who can you start referring business to?

New Markets with Niching and Repurposing

Most of this book has been about doing more with your existing customer base. Another option is finding NEW customer profiles or markets for your existing product portfolio.

For most of the first dozen years that I was running the Bay Area Mastermind, for example, we filled our groups exclusively with established business owners who were growing their business with a team.

These were business owners who were getting it done, taking action in their business, and seeing results. They had as much to share as they did to ask and this made for really great peer advisory groups.

Contrast that with early stage founders, who were just getting started for the first time, weren't yet scaling, and had more questions than expertise to share.

Whereas in our mastermind groups, our members would share what they were doing, what was working, and what was not working... our founders would have "how do I" questions.

These two groups don't mix well in a Mastermind group setting.

For years, when earlier stage founders would show interest in our Mastermind groups, we'd quickly disqualify them and invite them to come back when they had grown and were a better fit.

After quite a while of this, we realized that we were attracting a uniquely different market than our core customer base, and they were also looking for a Mastermind like group, but with more mentorship and advisory.

So with our existing list of prospects who were not qualified to do business with us... we launched a new program exclusively for earlier stage founders.

The two programs differed in a few important ways.

The first difference was the ideal member. They were two very distinct markets.

The second was the time commitment. Our mastermind group is a full-day meeting once a month for business owners who take that time out of the office to work *on* their business. Our founders group, by contrast, was a 90-minute meeting once a month as our founders were often still working jobs, didn't have as much knowledge to share, and spent more time on getting answers to their questions.

Lastly was the financial commitment. Our founders group had a considerably smaller financial commitment as these were folks getting off the ground and launching a new venture vs. established businesses with a budget for professional development.

This one same business added on a new offering to an adjacent - yet very distinct audience. This was almost an entirely new market and added a new revenue stream to the business.

Author Dan Kennedy famously does this with many of his books, by re-niching them with partners. One of his core books *Magnetic Marketing* has been republished again and again for niche audiences.

For example, there's Magnetic Marketing for Lawyers, Magnetic Marketing for Dentists, and so on.

Author Mike Michalowicz who wrote one of our favorite books, *Profit First*, has followed this same path with niched books like *Profit First for Creatives*, *Profit First for Minority Business Enterprises*, *Profit First for Contractors*, and so on.

The core content is the same, but the niche examples, and niche expert authority intro and commentary make it so much more valuable for a new market.

Put it into Action!

- Who are you attracting into your business that you don't currently serve?

- What could you do to serve that audience?

- Who else could use the same products and services you have to offer, but repositioned to be for their niche instead?

10. Fixing Your Broken Funnels

"The first step in solving a problem is to recognize that it does exist."
- Zig Ziglar

So while we can certainly focus on adding more suspects and prospects into the top of your funnel, you probably already have a funnel with customers coming out the end of it that's just not working as well as it could.

In simple terms a funnel is a one-way flow of people through a system in your business where at each progress step fewer people make it through.

In the world of Pay Per Click (PPC), this might look like ad impressions to clicks to opt-ins to purchases.

For content or SEO, this might look like searches, page views, opt-ins, and purchases.

As a final example, for email marketing, this might look like emails sent, opens, clicks, purchases.

Fixing up your broken funnels can take the exact same flow of leads that you have coming into your business and - without changing the funnel - increase the number of customers coming out the bottom. This in turn increases your Q!

But... How do we know how well - or not well - your funnel is performing?

And once you see where your funnels are failing, how do you fix them?

Where Your Funnel is Broken

Funnels typically have one of two problems, though only one of these issues is commonly looked at.

Funnels are either too leaky – i.e. conversions are low at a certain stage of the funnel.

Or... funnels are too effective – i.e. conversion is too HIGH at a step of the funnel. Yep, you read that right. A funnel that converts too highly is also a problem to be addressed.

Before we dive into fixing your funnel, let's go over your funnel stages and how to track them. Then we'll know where the problems are and what to fix.

Tracking Your Funnel Stages

You naturally want as many leads as possible heading into your funnel, but if they're not the *right* leads, you're going to have a leaky funnel. You want *qualified* prospects coming into your funnel – but not *overly* qualified leads.

In order to start diagnosing your funnel, you first need to track your funnel effectiveness.

If you're using a CRM and have built in reports or are using a tool like Google Analytics, that's wonderful. If not, just use a spreadsheet.

Add a row for each step of your funnel.

Next to the name for each step of your funnel, put the number of contacts that converted at that step.

Now you can calculate three key numbers for each row.

First, what percent of people from the previous step made it to this step.

Second, what percent of people from the top of the funnel made it to this step.

Third, what it cost for each person to get to that step.

For a super simple example, let's say my funnel is to get opt-ins to then schedule a call with me. My funnel might look something like this:

- Person Sees Ad (i.e. Impressions)

    - Cost is "Cost per Impression", i.e. total Ad Spend divided by impressions.

- Person Clicks Ad and sees Landing Page (i.e. Clicks)

    - Conversion rate is "Click Through Rate" aka CTR, i.e. Clicks divided by Impressions.

    - Cost is "Cost per Click" aka CPC, i.e. total Ad Spend divided by Clicks.

- Person Opts In (Hooray, a Lead!)

    - Conversion rate is Opt-Ins divided by Clicks.

    - Cost is "Cost per Lead" aka CPL, i.e. total Ad Spend divided by Leads.

- Lead Schedules Call (Hooray, hopefully a qualified lead!)

- Conversion rate is Calls Scheduled divided by Opt Ins

- Same math as the previous step. Cost is Ad Spend divided by Calls Scheduled.

  - Lead Shows Up For Call (Hooray, even more qualified!)

    - Conversion rate is Calls divided by Calls Scheduled. This is your "Show Rate"

    - Same math as previous step. Cost is Ad Spend divided by Calls.

  - Sale! Lead Buys on Call (Hooray, a Customer!)

    - Conversion rate is Sales divided by Calls.

    - Cost is "Cost per Acquisition" aka CPA, i.e. Ad Spend divided by Sales.

    - Your "Return on Investment" (ROI) or "Return on Ad Spend" (RoAS) is the monetary amount of your Sales divided by your Ad Spend.

What might these numbers look like? We'll return to these stages in a bit and go through the math – and the opportunities.

Finding Your Funnel Metrics

So where do you find these numbers?

If you're like some business owners I've worked with, you may not know *where* these numbers are, or if you do, you're probably not tracking them all in one place.

Until you have all of your numbers in one place, it's going to be challenging to track how effective your funnel is - and what change if any your tests have on patching your leaky funnel.

You can find your Ad Spend, Impressions, Clicks, and Goal Conversions in your ad tool like Google AdWords, Facebook Ad Manager, etc.

You can find page views or impressions as well as goal conversions in tools like Google Analytics.

You can find your sales numbers, stats, and other metrics in your e-commerce platform or CRM.

Leaky Funnels (i.e. Low Conversion)

The most common issue with a funnel is that it's leaky. People are dropping out at a step in the funnel and not moving forward to the next step.

Your conversions are lower than you'd like. This typically happens for one of a few reasons.

Funnel Stage Continuity

The first thing we typically do is look at continuity; in other words, how natural and sensible is it for a person to move from the previous step to the next?

If you're offering a book download opt-in and the thank you page is to book a call with you... you don't have continuity. It's an offer, but it's a pivot from the previous step.

If you're asking someone to apply for a call with you, and they opt-in, completing the application has high continuity and will have higher conversion. And naturally, then booking a call with you is the thing they've wanted to do all along and will have high continuity.

If you're offering a free lead magnet for an opt-in, and then immediately trying to make a high ticket sale, there is low continuity. You brought someone in with an offer for free and then immediately pivoted to asking for a high ticket sale.

Continuity also comes into play with look and feel, i.e. does your landing page match the design, style, and brand through each step of your funnel?

We've commonly seen a highly polished, pretty landing page and then the confirmation or upsell page looks drastically different. Oops.

Funnel Stage Follow Up

The second big thing we look for is follow up, in other words, how well do you help someone who dropped out of the funnel get back in.

For example, if you have a low show rate to your scheduled phone calls, are your contacts getting a reminder about the call? A calendar invite that automatically shows up on their calendar? An SMS text message reminder (with their permission)? An email reminder?

If your conversion rate from opt-in to purchase is low, do you have follow up emails to nurture your prospects and bring them back into your sales funnel?

If your upsell rate is low, do you have a marketing strategy to help your new customers along their customer journey with an opportunity to come back and take you up on your upsell offer?

Top of Funnel (ToFu) Lead Quality

The third big thing we look for is lead quality at the top of the funnel.

How qualified are the leads coming in?

Very often – especially with Pay Per Click (PPC) advertising – poor targeting means the wrong leads getting into your funnel.

For example, at the Bay Area Mastermind, we make it clear that our Mastermind is specifically for entrepreneurs with existing businesses that are generating sales of between $500k and $8mm a year and have a team in place supporting the business owner.

We specifically are not for people working a J.O.B. ("Just Over Broke"), pre-revenue startups with an idea but no sales, or solopreneurs who don't have at least one other person helping out in the business.

Even with that copy in place, when mis-targeted ads were run by agencies, we'd see leads come in that would leave a Gmail or Yahoo address for their email (not an established business owner), type their names in ALL CAPS (why are they yelling?), and then not even complete their Mastermind Application. Those were some very *low quality* leads.

Even though the Cost Per Click (CPC) may have been low(ish), and the Click Through Rate (CTR) was high, the lead quality was garbage and the Cost Per QUALIFIED Lead was outrageously high.

The Ad Agency thought they were doing a great job because of the low CPCs and high CTRs but the quality was *terrible*.

This is why you need to track each step of the funnel to see where lead quality starts to show.

Overly Effective Funnels

So what if your funnel is incredible and you're converting at 100%? Is that a good thing?

Let's say you have a hotel. Do you want 100% occupancy all the time? What does it mean if you're always full?

It means you could have been charging more. You could have been more discerning in your customers and just taken in better guests who cost less, who spend more, and are more enjoyable to work with.

It's the same thing with the funnels in your business.

A 100% conversion probably means you are over qualifying your leads and missing out on qualified leads who got rejected from your funnel too early. Or... you're not charging enough. (See Increasing your Prices!)

You're leaving money on the table.

If 100% of your clicks opt in, you're probably targeting your ads too narrowly and missing out on prospective customers.

If 100% of your sales calls convert to a customer, you're probably screening out too many prospects.

If 100% of your prospects buy, you are probably charging too little.

If 100% of your customers in your sales funnel take you up on your upsell, you could likely increase the price, add a more premium upsell, and/or add additional upsells after the first.

In one of my client's businesses, we were debating a price change for their subscription. They were priced at $19/mo and were considering a change to $29/mo. That's over 50% more in recurring revenue per customer.

But... Would they lose more than a third of their customers and acquire only two thirds as many customers going forward?

All else being equal, would you rather have, say 10,000 customers paying you $100/mo? Or 5,000 customers paying you $200/mo? It's $1,000,000/mo either way in revenue.

But the cost to support each customer is the same.

So your overall expenses are lower per customer (think support, service, fulfillment, onboarding, etc). AND, you can now spend MORE to get a customer.

So which would you prefer? Fewer higher paying customers for the same thing? Or more lower paying customers?

Funnels and the Newsvendor Problem

Effective funnels are related to the "Newsvendor Problem".

The Newsvendor Problem (or "Newsboy Problem" as it was called, because... 19th century) has to do with how many newspapers a newsstand should purchase for sale on a given day.

Purchase too many and all the extras are worthless the next day and a waste of money. You had too much *supply* for the *demand*.

Purchase too *few* newspapers and you've lost revenue because there's demand and you have no supply.

With your funnels, if you over qualify your prospects, you've lost revenue from prospects who might have been a good fit but got kicked out. There was more demand than you see.

If you under qualify your prospects, you'll have a leaky funnel with prospects who don't end up buying. The actual demand was far less than the expected demand.

Either way, you're losing customers and money.

Fixing Your Broken Funnels

Using the strategies above, you've now identified your conversion rate at each stage of the funnel.

You can now see which funnel stage has the biggest drop off and which conversions are the easiest to fix.

Some common fixes to broken funnels:

- Are your leads dropping out of your buying process? Can you add in lead nurturing? Specifically, an autoresponder sequence / marketing automation of follow up emails to bring your leads back into the funnel.

- Do you have buyers, but you're not getting enough customer testimonials? When and where do you ask for customer feedback? If you're not asking for testimonials, could you? If you are, can you ask in a different way or at a different stage?

- Is your sales process not converting more customers from the awareness stage of the funnel? Could you provide more value upfront with the right marketing messages?

- Is your paid advertising (i.e. paid ads like PPC for paid search leads) generating leads, but the leads are poor quality so you're not follow up marketing qualified leads? Could you better define your audience?

- Are you using content marketing to generate impressions, but the visitors aren't opting in to become leads? Are you using google analytics to better understand your visitors, where they're coming from, and what their level of purchase intent is? Do you create content based on the avatar of the customers you want? Have you done consumer research to better understand your target audience? Are you able to create an emotional connection with your prospects all the way through your marketing funnels?

- Are your marketing channels generating traffic, but the quality is low? Do you know where your traffic is coming from and what your visitors are doing on your site?

- Are you not even tracking your conversions at the different stages of your funnel? Can you use your CRM or even just a spreadsheet to start dashboarding your numbers?

- Is your buying process confusing because there's no continuity? Could your marketing campaign stay on the same message from the start of the customer's journey all the way through to purchase?

- Are your new leads opting in but then not buying? Can you use email marketing to follow up with your leads and present the right offer at the right time?

- Are your current customers buying one time, but not again? Could you create a follow up marketing to get positive customer reviews, gauge customer satisfaction, create loyal customers, and bring customers back for additional purchases?

- Are you trying to increase sales but your potential customers bail after opting in? How congruent is your content from the top of your funnel all the way through? Do you have continuity from your ad to your landing page to your thank you page to your offer?

Once we make one change, we measure the impact that has on the funnel step addressed.

If we like the result, we keep it and move on to fixing our next worst performing part of the funnel and repeat.

Just like the British Cycling Team from our chapter on Revenue Multipliers, we're looking for even the smallest 1% improvement in our funnel.

Every little bit counts. Making just a 1% change at a time, has that compounding effect that Einstein and others so loved.

Funnel Tracking Spreadsheet

From the funnel example I mentioned, where you're running ads to book sales calls, what might a tracking sheet look like?

Using the stages above and a simple Google Sheet, you might have something like this:

Step	#	% of Top	% of Previous	Cost Per	Value Per
Impression	8,417	100%		$0.14	$0.19
Clicks	151	2%		$8.06	$10.58
Opt-Ins	13	0.2%	9%	$94	$123
Schedules Call	11	0.1%	85%	$111	$145
Shows Up for Call	4	0.0%	31%	$304	$400
Purchases	2	0.0%	50%	$609	$799
Ad Spend	$1,217				
Total Sales	$1,598				
RoAS	131.31%				

Get a free copy of this spreadsheet along with some other great tools online at YourBusinessGrowthPlaybook.com under Bonuses.

With a total Ad Spend of $1,217 and two sales of $799 each (for a total of $1,598), we can see a number of important things.

First, our Return on Ad Spend (RoAS) is 131%. Not bad. For every $100 you spend, you'll get $131 back. And that's just on the first sale and doesn't consider total Customer Lifetime Value (CLV) or future sales.

Second, we can reverse calculate the value of each step, for example, we know that for everyone who purchases, they cost $609 and spent $799.

But going back up the funnel, we can also see that, for each person who shows up for a call, it costs $304 and is worth $400.

And for each person who opts in, the opt-in is worth $123 and only cost $94.

So... where are the opportunities in this funnel?

The click through rate isn't bad, but the opt-in rate is a little low. Only 9% of people who are interested in the ad are actually opting in. That could likely be improved with better continuity from ad copy to landing page and from targeting to offer.

Second, the show up rate for calls is pretty low. Only 31% of people who schedule a call actually show up for the call. That could speak to lead quality or a lack of proper follow up to get the person on the call, i.e. sending a calendar invite, sending a permission based SMS reminder, etc.

Let's say we fix those two items above and we get twice as many people to show up for their calls bumping the show rate from 31% to 62% and bumping the opt-in rate from 9% to 17%.

How does fixing the lead quality, continuity and follow up affect our numbers?

Let's take a look.

Step	#	% of Top	% of Previous	Cost Per	Value Per
Impression	8,417	100%		$0.14	$0.76
Clicks	151	2%		$8.06	$42.33
Opt-Ins	26	0.3%	17%	$47	$246
Schedules Call	22	0.3%	85%	$55	$291
Shows Up for Call	16	0.2%	62%	$76	$400
Purchases	8	0.1%	50%	$152	$799
Ad Spend	$1,217				
Total Sales	$6,392				
RoAS	525.23%				

First of all, we've just grown our overall sales four times over... which does the same for our RoAS.

Secondly, the VALUE of our previous steps increases. And the COST per step decreases.

Your same ad spend now gets you $525 for every $100 you spend. WOAH.

And now, when someone clicks, you know their value is $42, up from $10. And when they schedule their call, they're worth $291, up from $145. Even better, your cost per opt-in is now $47, down from $94, and your cost per phone conversation is $76, down from $304!

Putting it all together, fixing your funnels really comes down to these steps:

1. Know your funnel steps and actual numbers at each stage of the funnel, like have an actual spreadsheet or dashboard.

2. Calculate your cost per, conversion rate, and overall conversion rate for each step of your funnel, like have those numbers calculated in your spreadsheet or dashboard.

3. At the funnel stages where your conversion rates are too low or too high, look at what you can do to improve lead quality (with

qualification/disqualification), continuity, and follow-up.

Start tracking your funnel stats. Look for the opportunities. Fix them.

11. Bonus: Decreasing the Amount of Each Transaction?

"Price is what you pay. Value is what you get." - Warren Buffet

The inverse of increasing the amount of each transaction is the fallacy of discounts. Discounts are disastrous to your business!

"20% Off!" "Buy One, Get One Free!", "Black Friday Sale!" "... Going Out of Business!"

Your discount promotions are gutting your business – and you might not even know it.

We see promotions all the time where companies discount their products and services, but those businesses never share what that actually means financially behind the scenes – and why it leads so many businesses to, through desperation, lay off staff or close up shop entirely.

Promotions can begin a business' death spiral, delay consumer purchases, and put you out of business before you even realize it.

Let's take a look at both the consumer behavior of discounting as well as the cold hard truth of the financials behind discounting. And lastly, let's go over a few key strategies that can get the same perceived benefits of discounting - without actually discounting.

The Financial Toll of Discounting Your Products

Ready to dive into the nerdy numbers of business and see what discounts do to your company's financials?

Pull out your trusty Profit and Loss Statement (P&L), look at your actual numbers and follow along with a few easy examples.

We introduced this example at the start of the book, so this may look familiar. But now we're going to dive even deeper into these numbers.

Let's say you have $4mm in Gross Revenue.

And your Cost of Goods Sold (CoGS, what those sales cost you) is $1mm (25%).

Your Gross Profit is $4mm – $1mm = $3mm (75%).

Let's say your business expenses are $2.5mm (62.5%).

That leaves you with a Net Profit of $500k (12.5%). Not bad.

The Impact of Discounting 10%

Now let's say you decide to run a limited promotion, perhaps a mere 10% off sale....

You now have $3.6mm in Gross Revenue.

Your CoGS is the same at $1mm (25% -> 27.7%)

But... your Gross Profit takes a hit (75% -> 72.2%)

And since your expenses are also the same at $2.5mm... (62.5% -> 69.4%)

This brings your Net Profit down from $400k to $100k! (12.5% -> 2.7%)

Yeah, you just lost 75% of your profit.

That's scarily barely profitable!

The Impact of a 15% Discount...

Using the same example numbers above, a discount of 15% get us:

$3.4mm in Gross Revenue

-$1mm CoGS (same)

-$2.5mm in Expenses (same)

= -$100k (NEGATIVE One Hundred Thousand) in Gross Profit

THIS is how many businesses start their death spiral out of business. You can NOT discount your way to profitability!

What if Discounting Increases Your Quantity of Sales?

Okay, so let's say you want to argue that discounting your products will increase your quantity of sales...

Maybe. But remember, with increased sales volume, your Cost of Goods Sold (CoGS) increases, too.

So let's say that your 15% discount promotion increases your sales volume and your gross sales stay the same as without discounts at $4mm...

Your CoGS, however, increases - because of sales volume - to $1.2mm. (See, we keep the same CoGS percentage of 29.4% from our previous calculation with a 15% discount.)

Gross Profit rebounds to $2.8mm with the same percentage of 71% from our previous calculation, too.

But Expenses stay the same. So our Net Profit ends up at $300k - or only 8.1%.

Still profitable, but less profitable than if you hadn't discounted in the first place!

Now keep in mind, this is all because you're discounting an initial one-time purchase with no other benefit than just getting a sale. This is *not* the same as offering a discount to reward loyal customers that buy from you again or that subscribe to recurring purchases.

Mega Discount! Double Your Sales! (...?)

Let's say you ratchet your discount up to 40% off and that leads to a huge increase of sales (almost DOUBLE) so you're now grossing $4.5mm. Your CoGS also almost doubles to $1.8mm (42%!!!). Your Gross Profit is down to $2.6mm. And your Net Profit is a mere $125k... or 2.8%.

Take a look at what happened to Wahoo at the end of 2022. Among other problems, they ran some pretty steep promos during the holiday season to move inventory.

S&P Global Ratings, who lowered their financial rating, said of this: "...the promotional activities to manage its elevated inventory levels, including Cyber Week discounts, continue to drag on its profitability. Therefore, we expect the company will report negative EBITDA in 2022. In addition, we do not expect Wahoo will be able to significantly improve its profitability and cash flow..."

And now what happens when your customers see you running promotions and discounts? What does that do to their behavior?

Let's look into the behavioral psychology of your buyer who knows you run promotions and sales...

The Psychological Impact of Discounting

Psychologically, to your customers, when they see you discount your product, a few questions come up for them.

You've asked yourself these very same questions before as a consumer.

Have you waited to buy something because you knew Black Friday was around the corner or a Super Bowl promo was likely coming up?

Perhaps you held off on buying that new TV for a few weeks or a month knowing a predictable deal would be around the corner. Or you held off on buying a new appliance knowing a holiday promo was coming up.

Or how about travel costs. Have you ever been frustrated when you found out someone paid less for the same airline ticket that you bought, or got a better deal on the same car than you did?

Your customers have these exact same thoughts and feelings.

When your customers see a promotion for something they were considering buying – or recently bought – they ask "If they [your company] can sell this to me at this discount, why were they overcharging me before?"

And secondly, the next time they want to buy from you, they wonder "Why should I buy now, if I know there will be a discount coming up?"

Back to Black Friday... "Over 70% of consumers indicate that they believe the best deals of the year are found during the holiday shopping season."

If you're shopping with a brand that you know doesn't play that game, however, you buy for other reasons that are not discount related.

Take REI, for example, and their #OptOutside movement:

"Since 2015, we've closed our doors on Black Friday, choosing time outside over the busiest in-store shopping day of the year."

REI customers know not to wait to buy and not to expect a discount. They buy when they want the product they need and for other motivating reasons that we cover further on under strategies below.

Lastly, if you have a premium priced product (and you certainly should), discounting it hurts the perceived value and makes justifying your regular pricing far more difficult. More on luxury marketing in a moment.

People tend to take your discounted price into account and "anchor" that as the actual value of your product or service in the future. Customers now value your product at the discounted price and most people will take that price into account when making future purchase decisions.

They expect you to be selling at the sale price forever forward. They determine the price they *expect* to pay in the later on based on your *present* day promotion.

Increasing Sales without Discounting

The reason you probably planned to run a promotion and discount your products and services was that you wanted to increase sales. You can get the same bump in sales, however, without discounting.

Increased Value in Promotions

You can always add in more value to your offering or promotion – value that is *greater* to your customer than the *cost* to you.

This is especially prevalent in luxury brand marketing. For example, the addition of an exclusive free gift with purchase for a limited time only or while supplies last.

Your luxury buyer isn't looking for a deal as much as they're looking for status. How can you help them show their status?

Adding in a limited time free personalization or customization can increase the value of what you're selling without discounting.

Offer exclusive access to a private members only community just for your customers and clients. This could be as simple as a private Facebook group, a Slack team, or a Discord channel.

You can offer perks or points, like induction to a VIP Buyer club or a Silver, Gold, Platinum level.

Back to REI above. They have a co-op that us members – not customers – buy into. That is also a loyalty program. With points. Add a credit card that gets you points. And additional exclusive members perks.

Zappos famously created a VIP Buyer program that provided a few perks like free shipping. Getting in was as simple as making a purchase – or asking for membership. But the exclusivity and perks kept buyers coming back and buying more.

And while we're talking about Luxury Marketing, rewind back in this article to the comment about "anchor pricing". Luxury buyers looking for status and exclusivity often see more value in a higher price point. Simply adding in a higher priced package or offer can help you both to sell more of the package you do want to sell AND, as a bonus, you'll start getting a few much more profitable higher end sales, too.

One of our Mastermind members used this to his advantage when selling coaching programs.

Initially given the choice between a $10k/year and a $30k/year coaching program, many of his buyers would purchase the $10k program. Simply by adding in a $75k/year coaching program, he saw an increased number of buyers for the (now mid-tier) $30k/year program. AND, as expected, he acquired a select few new high end clients in the $75k/year program – moreover, these were high end buyers who never would have bought the $30k/year program!

Scarcity and Urgency in Promotions

Fake scarcity is dumb, insincere, and possibly even fraudulent. Real scarcity, however, is a very effective motivator.

We've all felt FoMO (Fear of Missing Out) before.

Because we've missed out. And that sucks. Think about:

- When it's holiday time and the latest hot holiday gift is out of stock and you didn't get it before everyone else did.

- When the airline price you were considering is now gone.

- When the concert tickets you wanted were all sold within minutes of going on sale.

- When that hot stock you were thinking about hockey-sticked before you could buy it.

And on and on.

What is actually *limited* in your business?

Do you take phone consultations? Your calendar only has so much space.

Does your team service your clients? There's only so much availability for new clients.

Do you sell physical products? There are only so many in inventory.

Does your product use a limited quantity of difficult to source ingredients? There's only so many you can make.

One of our Mastermind members handles physical system installs for businesses. Before putting proper systems in place, they were responding to requests the same or next day, not getting signed contracts, footing the bill for goods, and having a hard time collecting payment months later.

After our work together, and with proper systems in place to handle new business, however, and real proper scarcity on their calendar, they began booking business 2+ months out, collecting deposits up front before buying hardware, getting signed contracts, and getting paid. All without discounting.

One of our other Mastermind members has an online supplement business and creates a limited run of special hand crafted products from time to time. These are premium priced and very limited in quantity due to their ingredients. These sell out every single time they are released. Because of scarcity. All without discounting.

Where is the real scarcity in your business?

Have you highlighted that to your customers?

12. Bonus: Expense Reduction

We can't talk about increasing your profitability without at least touching on the important topic of Expense Reduction.

Increasing your gross sales grows your *top line*, but if we want to improve your *bottom line*, we can also reduce what you're spending in the business.

There's no better expert in the expense reduction space than my client and friend, Marc Freedman. After four decades of helping over 25,000 businesses reduce their expenses, he published an entire book on the topic, *Expense To Profit: Eliminate The Costs That Sabotage Your Growth*.

His work is typically with some of the largest businesses on the planet and he's helped them reduce their expenses by literally *billions* of dollars. (His largest client has ~15 *billion* dollars a year in expenses...)

Now, while most of his strategies may apply to significantly larger businesses, many of the cost categories exist in *your* business, too. The same techniques he uses to help big business can often be applied at a smaller scale, too.

There are over 40 notable expense categories rife for reduction that almost all businesses have. You're probably overpaying for certain categories of products or services in your business.

For the purposes of this book and our dear readers, I interviewed Marc about expense reduction specifically for smaller businesses. This was our conversation:

Marc Freedman on Expense Reduction

Jeremy: Our audience consists of smaller business owners. These businesses generate revenue and have teams in place, but they're not the large global corporations you typically work with. However, I know there's still a good overlap in strategies.

Marc: Absolutely! The ideas remain the same. Plus, I also have a partner who works with smaller businesses, so that may be an option as well.

Jeremy: Excellent! I also understand that many strategies and approaches are similar, just at a different scale.

You often talk about the 40 major categories of expenses where businesses can typically save money. Some of these might apply more to global companies, but for smaller businesses in the sub-$5mm to $10mm range, what are some top categories where they can cut costs?

Marc: One major category is **health insurance**. When we ask business owners which check they hate writing the most every month, it's usually the one to the insurance company. These costs tend to rise 7% to 15% each year, often without justification.

One way to handle this is to have a conversation with your insurance agent or policy manager. You might not have access to your claims history, but if you know your employees rarely take time off due to medical issues, that's worth bringing up. Simply asking underwriters if there's room to lower costs can sometimes yield results.

This principle applies to any vendor. You can call and say, "I love doing business with you, but I have another opportunity. I'd hate for our relationship to end—what can you do to help lower these costs?"

Vendors raised prices during the pandemic simply because they could. Our goal is to bring businesses back to market price.

Jeremy: That makes sense. So, insurance - especially health insurance - is a major expense. Is the solution typically to pass costs onto employees through higher premiums, or is it about negotiating with providers?

Marc: There are several approaches. Some businesses raise deductibles or copays to reduce costs. But if your goal is to avoid making employees pay more, a strategy is to cover employees 100% while having them pay extra for spouses or families.

Since many households have dual incomes, employees might already have coverage through their spouse's employer. The fewer people covered, the lower the risk of catastrophic claims that can drive up costs.

Another big area where businesses can save is **wireless services.** Many people don't realize they can negotiate lower wireless bills. Switching providers based on coverage can be an option, but sometimes simply calling your carrier can get results. I personally use both Verizon and AT&T on my phone, switching based on location.

For example, I once noticed my AT&T bill had unexpectedly increased. After calling them, I found they had changed something in their system, automatically raising my rate. I told them I would leave unless they fixed it. Initially, they resisted, but after escalating to customer retention, my bill was restored to the original amount.

Many times, a simple phone call can save you money.

Jeremy: That's great advice! So, beyond health insurance and telecom, what are some other major categories where businesses can cut costs?

Marc: Other common areas include:

1. **Payroll & Worker's Compensation:** Switching to a "pay-as-you-go" model for workers' compensation can provide a 15% discount and eliminate year-end audits.

2. **Rent & Office Space:** Many businesses pay for more space than they need. Given the current market, landlords don't want to lose tenants. You can negotiate lower rent or reduce your leased space. Even in shared office spaces, requesting a lower increase than proposed can work.

3. **Utilities (Electricity & Gas):** If you're in a deregulated state, you can shop for electricity and gas providers. Working with an energy broker can help you secure a lower rate.

Jeremy: That's insightful. How should business owners identify the easiest cost-saving opportunities for their specific businesses?

Marc: Start with your **biggest expenses** first because that's where the most meaningful reductions can be made.

Typically, we find businesses are overspending by about **18% on their top 3-5 expenses.**

For example, if a business has $5mm in expenses (with $2.5M of that being payroll), saving 18% on the $2.5M of non-payroll expenses could mean $450K in savings.

That's a significant amount that could be reinvested into the business.

Jeremy: What do businesses typically do once they free up that extra 18%?

Marc: It depends. Some reinvest in growth—buying leads, hiring new employees, or expanding operations. Others use the savings to increase salaries, provide bonuses, or pay themselves for the first time in a while.

Jeremy: What are some common mistakes business owners make when trying to reduce expenses?

Marc: The biggest mistake is assuming long-term vendor relationships guarantee the best pricing.

We often hear things like, "We've been doing business with them for 85 years; of course, they're giving us the best rates."

However, we frequently find companies overpaying by millions because they never check pricing.

You need to **compare vendor rates regularly**.

Vendors know market pricing, so don't throw out round numbers when negotiating—use odd figures like 17% or 18% instead of 20% to sound more credible.

Jeremy: When should businesses actually switch vendors versus negotiating with their current provider?

Marc: 95% of the time, we recommend staying with the existing vendor and negotiating lower prices.

Switching vendors is disruptive—new systems, new contacts, new terms. Only in extreme cases, where the savings justify the transition, should businesses switch.

For instance, **changing health insurance providers** is easier than many think. Most major providers (Blue Cross, United Healthcare, Cigna, Aetna) contract with the same doctors.

Before switching, check if your employees' doctors are covered under the new plan.

Jeremy: How often should businesses reassess their expenses?

Marc: Expense reduction should be an **ongoing process.**

Ideally, businesses should secure **two- to three-year contracts** for price stability. Reviewing expenses every **12 to 24 months** helps keep costs in check.

One example: A dental business we worked with had a **handshake agreement** for a "cost-plus-15%" pricing model on medical supplies.

When we audited their expenses, we found they were overpaying by **18%**—simply because they never defined what "cost" meant in their contract.

Jeremy: That's a powerful example. What about credit card processing fees? Those seem to be another hidden expense.

Marc: Absolutely! Credit card processing fees are **highly negotiable.**

Many providers charge unnecessary fees—statement fees, transaction fees, etc. These can often be reduced or eliminated.

When I set up my own merchant account, I negotiated **2.68% flat** with no extra fees, instead of the **3.3% standard rate.**

Jeremy: That's great to know. Where can business owners learn more about expense reduction strategies?

Marc: Our website, , has blog articles and resources on cost-saving strategies. Business owners can also schedule a consultation with us for tailored advice.

Jeremy: I love how your site provides **timely updates** on industry changes, government regulations, and cost-saving opportunities.

Marc: Exactly! One of the big trends right now is **employee wellness programs,** which can save businesses **$600 per employee per year** while giving employees more benefits.

Jeremy: Thank you so much Marc

Expense Reduction Action Plan

So! What can you do right now to start reducing your expenses?

Here are five action items you can do today to start reducing expenses for your business:

Identify your top 3-5 spending categories.

Focusing on the areas where you spend the most money is the quickest path to finding significant savings. These areas usually offer the most "low-hanging fruit".

Call these vendors first and negotiate pricing.

Review your health insurance plan.

This is a major area where costs can often be reduced. Contact your insurance provider, and ask them if they can lower your costs. Specifically, have them review your claim history.

Check your telecom/wireless bills.

Call your providers and ask for a better rate. If they are unwilling to help, speak to their customer retention department. You may also want to consider if another provider is more affordable and offers better service in your area.

Assess your office space.

If you are paying rent, determine if you have too much space. If so, speak with your landlord about reducing your rent, and potentially giving back unused space.

Landlords may be willing to do this rather than lose you as a tenant. In addition, negotiate any rent increases.

Consider software deals.

Look for software deals offered on the products you use. You may also want to consider paying annually to get a discount, and explore opportunities for lifetime memberships.

These steps will help you quickly start finding areas where you can reduce expenses and increase the profitability of your business. By taking the first step and addressing these common expense categories, you'll gain valuable insights and experience for further cost optimization.

13. Prioritization - Do Now, Schedule, Delegate, Or Delete

"Plans are nothing; planning is everything." - Dwight Eisenhower

Now that you have your playbook of strategies to increase revenue and tactics for reducing expenses, you're almost ready to create your personalized Action Plan.

It's likely you're feeling a bit overwhelmed with all that you *could* or *should* do.

It can be hard to begin when you're not sure what THE priority is.

That's right priority *singular*, not priorities *plural*.

It's funny, the word "priority" (from the Latin *"prioritas,"*) was used in the late Middle Ages to denote some*thing* that was considered more important than *all* others.

It wasn't until World War II that General Dwight D. Eisenhower, who served as the Supreme Commander of the Allied Expeditionary Forces in Europe, and the 34th president of the United States, started using the plural form, "priorities" to refer to *multiple* objectives that were *most important.*

And it's thanks (hah!) to him that we now talk about our *priorities* plural. And we find ourselves with too many *most important* things to do.

Thankfully, Eisenhower *also* gave us a powerful decision making tool to figure out *what* of our gigantic to do lists should get done and when.

In fact, instead of just figuring out which items to move "up" or "down" on the list, Eisenhower had a matrix that he used to figure out far more than just the priority of an item. His Eisenhower Matrix helps us to figure out *who* is going to get something done, *when*, and if at *all*.

That last part's almost the most important, and we'll see why in a moment.

Choosing *what* to work on is what differentiates working hard and getting nowhere from working smart and scaling your business while working less.

Eisenhower credits his unusually high productivity with a simple quadrant system he created for organizing the tasks he needed to get done.

First, he categories each task as Urgent or Not Urgent.

Next, he decided if each task was Important or Not Important.

That helped him put each task into the correct quadrant of his matrix.

	URGENT	NOT URGENT
IMPORTANT	DO NOW	SCHEDULE
NOT IMPORTANT	DELEGATE	DELETE

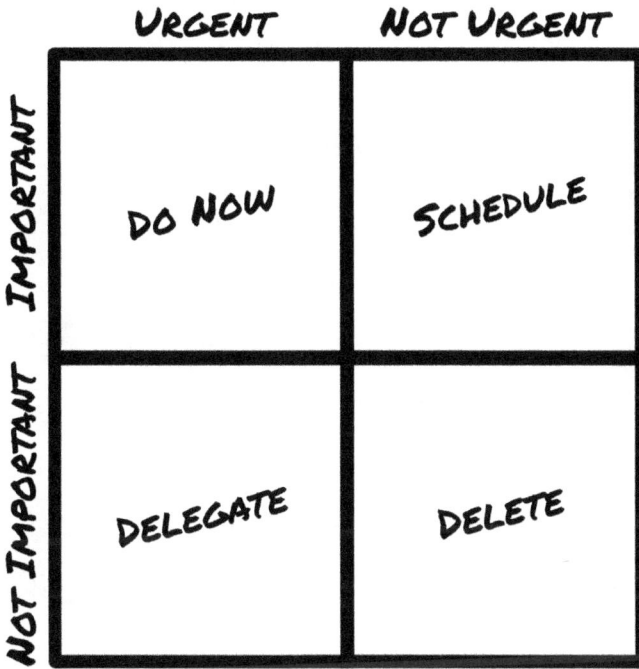

The Four Quadrants of the Eisenhower Matrix

Eisenhower put all of his urgent tasks on the left side and non-urgent tasks on the right side.

Then all of the important tasks went on the top and all of the non-important tasks went on the bottom.

This then placed each task into one of four quadrants:

- Important and Urgent tasks are in the top left

- Important and Non-Urgent tasks are in the top right

- Non-Important but Urgent tasks are on the bottom left

- Non-Important and Non-Urgent tasks are on the bottom right

What you'll find as you prioritize tasks using this task management tool is that each quadrant can be handled differently.

Important and Urgent Tasks

Your important and urgent tasks in the upper left are your fires that need to be put out.

In your business, you want to do as little firefighting as possible, but when fires do come up, they need to be dealt with.

If you find yourself constantly in firefighting mode, you're in survival mode and can't focus on growing the business.

Your important and urgent tasks just need to get done.

Important and Non-Urgent Tasks

The tasks in your top right quadrant are your Important and Non-Urgent tasks. These need to get done, but they're not fires. These are often the items that - due to not being urgent - get kicked down the road when you're firefighting.

Interestingly, the tasks in this quadrant are often the most important things that can help you grow your business - and have less fires to fight.

These may even be the projects that help you to have fewer fires in the first place: Tasks like creating your SOPs (Standard Operating Procedures), hiring, training, R&D (Research and Development for "what's next" in your business), and so on.

If you've found yourself, during the course of reading this book, thinking "I *want* to implement Jeremy's strategies in my business, but I just *don't have time!*" you're not alone. All of your great ideas you've been writing down likely fall in this quadrant.

Your important and non-urgent tasks should be scheduled and time blocked on your calendar so they get done.

Ideally, get these done first thing in the day before you get into firefighting.

Unimportant and Urgent Tasks

Tasks that don't actively help you towards your goals or towards growth but are urgent can be handled in one of two ways. Either have someone else do them so you can focus on what matters most, or see just how urgent they are and postpone if possible.

Many of these tasks are the work of and in the business that you shouldn't be doing in the first place, but someone else should be. Think about tasks like balancing your books, handling payroll, paying your taxes on time, flipping the proverbial burgers, etc.

The weight of a pressing deadline doesn't need to be your burden to bear alone.

Lastly, these seeming urgent issues are in fact seldom urgent. Filing your taxes, for example, is only urgent if you've procrastinated and failed to delegate.

Unimportant and Urgent Tasks should be delegated or postponed so you can stay focused.

Unimportant and Non-Urgent Tasks

The fourth quadrant includes the tasks that both don't need your immediate attention and are not that important.

This is the easiest category to deal with. Simply get rid of these items from your task list.

They don't matter.

They are a waste of your time.

These time-wasting activities are busy work at its worst.

Any time spent on these unnecessary tasks pulls you away from your time sensitive tasks.

Don't do your unimportant and non-urgent tasks!

Delegating Tasks - Who and How

So you've taken your ideas and your to do list and figured out which are your pressing problems that aren't that important. And now, you have to delegate, but to whom do you delegate?

If you don't already have a team member who you can offload the task to, this may be the right time to hire. This can be an outsourced hire, a vendor, an employee hire, or maybe even a task for a virtual assistant (VA) to help you out.

For some solopreneuers, often their first category of tasks outsourced is the bookkeeping, invoicing, and payroll. Other times, it may be appointment scheduling, copywriting, graphic design, support, or sales phone calls.

Hiring the right people is a solid Important Non-Urgent task that needs to get scheduled and done. Delegating tasks lets you "clone yourself" so you can focus on the tasks that matter most.

How to Rebalance Your Quadrants

Well done on organizing your tasks into quadrants!

What happens if you find they're grossly unbalanced and all of your items seem like urgent and important tasks needing your immediate attention?

Urgent and important tasks are your fires that need to be put out, but the same kinds of fires shouldn't keep coming up again and again. That would be a sign of a missing system in your business - or a lack of team to use the system properly.

As you put out a fire, put on your Important and Non-Urgent tasks a task to create a system to avoid that issue coming up again - or a task to hire someone to prevent or handle that kind of issue in the future.

If on the other hand, you find all of your tasks are important and non-urgent - and it stays that way - then it may be time to take a hard look at which of those many tasks are really important and which ones just seem important.

Clarity on your goals (or your bigger picture mission, vision, and purpose) can help you decide what's important vs a distraction.

So. With that in mind, let's jump into your Action Plan.

Remember, you don't need to be the one to actually *implement* all of these changes. But you *will* need to block the time to make these Important and Non-Urgent changes in your business.

14. Your Action Plan

Now you've seen the three big levers you can adjust in your business to impact gross revenues and profits.

And you're at a crossroads.

The good news is that you're the business owner and you can do whatever you want in your business.

The bad news is that you're the business owner and it's up to you to *decide* what you want to work on.

I've always found it interesting that the root of the word "decide" is from Old French *decider*, in turn from Latin *decidere* which combines *de* "off" and *caedere* "to cut".

Decide *literally* means "to cut off."

Deciding is less about choosing an option and more about all the other options you're saying no to at that time.

Indecision - the opposite of deciding - means not making a choice and in turn not doing anything.

As entrepreneurs, we take action. We decide. We move forward.

And now it's time for you to make a plan.

Which lever are you going to work on first?

Perhaps you want to start with increasing the Frequency of your transactions with subscriptions and new offerings?

Or maybe you want to focus first on increasing the Amount of your transactions with upsells and price increases?

On the other hand, you might not be doing enough on lead generation and want to start with increasing the Quantity of your transactions with more qualified leads?

The nice thing with an iterative process is that you get to repeat it again and again - ideally improving each step of the way.

Not every change you make is going to have a positive - or any - impact on your business. But you don't know which strategies will make the biggest impact until you try them out.

And that requires you to make a decision, measure the results, and then continue with that decision, try something else, or unwind your decision (if possible).

Every little experiment that you choose to run is a step forward. Either it makes a difference or you learn something from the experiment.

To get started with your action plan, let's start at the top.

You can download this action plan as an editable document online at *YourBusinessGrowthPlaybook.com* under Bonuses.

Your Products / Services

What are your main products and services that you have to offer? And what do you charge?

What bundles or packages do you offer that combine your items above?

As you look at your price points, when did you last raise your prices?

Why did you choose the prices listed?

What is the *value* of each of your products or services to your customers?

What price changes could you experiment with to increase the Amount of each transaction when a customer purchases?

How could offering a payment plan or third party financing help you to increase your prices or get more customers?

What gifts or tiered bonuses could you offer customers at time of purchase to encourage a larger transaction?

In what ways could you offer paid personalization or customization to your customers at time of purchase for a fee?

Where would it make sense to offer volume or prepaid discounts to encourage a larger up front purchase with you?

When customers are purchasing your top products above, what else could you offer them at that time to increase the value of what they're getting? ("Would you like fries with that?")

Adding in and improving your upsells will help you to increase the Amount of your initial Transaction.

What subscriptions, membership, continuity, or SaaS could you offer your customer base to add in more recurring revenue?

Your Ideal Customer

Who is your ideal customer? Really specifically, who are they? Let's break that down into a really specific list.

What are the top 12 mistakes that your prospects make?

1.

2.

3.

4.

5.

6.

7.

8.

9.

10.

11.

12.

Next up, describe your ideal customer's demographics, psychographics, like how old are they? Where do they live? How do they live? What are they like? What are their hobbies? How do they vote? Are they married, signal, separated, widowed? Do they have kids or grandkids? What books or magazines do they read? What radio / podcasts / shows do they enjoy? What keeps them up at night? What are their beliefs around money? What are their religious beliefs? What do they value? What frustrates them? And so on.

We're looking for a list of 23 items here. The first 5 will be easy. And then it'll become more difficult. That's okay. This is meant to stretch you.

1.

2.

3.

4.

5.

6.

7.

8.

9.

10.

11.

12.

13.

14.

15.

16.

17.

18.

19.

20.

21.

22.

23.

If you had to pick just 7 items from your list above that best identify your ideal customer, which 7 would they be? Put a star next to those.

Now, if you had to give your ideal customer avatar a name, what would it be? Think of this customer as an actual person that you're going to be writing a letter to. Who would you address it to? Bob? Natasha? Maria? Elwin? You pick the name.

Take a look at your advertising, marketing, and follow up. How well are you speaking directly to this avatar? What could you do better?

Improving how you connect with your avatar will help you to increase the Quantity of customers.

What other avatars / niches could use your *same products and services* just better tailored to them?

Your Funnel

Next up, let's look at how you're getting your customers.

How are you getting your customers? Specifically, what are your main lead sources?

- Pay Per Click (PPC)

  ◦ Facebook PPC

  ◦ Google AdWords

  ◦ Bing

  ◦ Amazon Ads

- ○ Yelp

- ○ Other:

- Organic Online (SEO)

- Marketplaces (i.e. Yelp, Etsy, Amazon, etc)

- Referral Partners

- Affiliates

- Direct Mail

- Cold Outbound Emailing

- Cold Calling / Telemarketing

- Social Media

- Media / Press / Podcasts / PR

- Other:

Where aren't you getting customers from the list above that you could be? Circle 3 new channels you want to experiment with to generate new customers.

How will you define success for these new channels?

What can you do *today* to get started in using these new channels?

Who is going to be in charge of getting you to success in each of these new channels? Will it be you? A team member? A vendor? An agency? A freelancer?

Once a prospect finds out about you, what are the specific funnel steps to get them to become a paid customer? (We'll come back to source and quantity in a moment, you can leave those blank for now)

See our chapter on Tracking Your Funnel Stages for some examples of common funnel steps.

Funnel Step | Stat Source | Quantity

Where do you find each of these numbers in your systems?

For example, do you find this stat in your CRM? In your Google Analytics? In your Ad platform?

Fill in your Stat Source for each funnel step.

Lastly, now that you know the stat sources, what are the numbers currently for each of your funnel steps? This can be for whatever time frame makes sense, just use the same timeframe for all the stats. For example, you can look at just last month, the previous 7 days, all of last year, whatever feels right.

Fill those in under the Quantity column.

With your baseline numbers filled in, let's look at our conversion rate for each step.

What do you call each step of the conversion, for example, from Impression to Click would be "Click Through Rate", from Page View to Opt-In would be Opt-In Rate.

See our chapter on Tracking Your Funnel Stages for more ideas on these steps and their conversion names.

Your rate is then the number at that step divided by the previous step. So, if you had 1,000 page views and 20 opt-ins, your Opt-In Rate would be 20/1,000 or 2%.

Conversion Step Name | Conversion Rate

Looking at your conversion rates, what are your worst ones of the bunch? Rank them with a 1, 2, and a 3.

What are 3 strategies you can use to improve each one of those conversion rates?

When customers fall out of your funnel at the point of purchase, what downsells could you offer them?

Who are your biggest suppliers? Which of these suppliers in your supply chain might be a good business for you to buy or replace as you work your way up your supply chain?

These strategies above will all help you to increase your Quantity of Customers.

Your Customer Lifetime Value

After your customers make their initial purchase from you, what else do they typically purchase from you?

How many times does a customer typically transact with you right now in total over their lifetime?

What is the average dollar (or Euro, whatever) amount that your customers currently spend with you right now on each transaction?

Multiplying these numbers together, what is your current Customer Lifetime Value (CLV)?

$$\underline{\hspace{2cm}} \times \underline{\hspace{3cm}} = \underline{\hspace{2cm}}$$
Frequency x Amount = CLV

If you don't currently offer a recurring revenue service or subscription, what might it look like if you did? What could customers purchase from you automatically weekly / monthly / annually? How much would they pay for that?

If you *do* currently have a recurring revenue component to your business, how many tiers of membership / service do you have and what are they? (Like Bronze, Silver, Gold, or... Basic, VIP, Platinum, etc)

What does your churn look like? What percentage of your members started a month / year with you and then cancel / lapse during that time period?

What could you do to reduce your churn?

What offers could you put in place in your business for each of the 4 cancellation categories? (See our chapter on Reducing Churn)

What is your current ladder of ascension - if you have one - from lowest end purchase to highest end purchase that customers typically make? (Note that this is different from the product portfolio question. This is about a linear path of purchases)

What else can you add to your funnel either before, after, or between your existing ladder steps above? Like, what other products or add-on services could you offer that would bring value to your customers?

If you have an affiliate program, what can you be doing to recruit more affiliates and encourage more business from your existing affiliates? Do you have an affiliate manager to oversee this all for you?

If you don't yet have an affiliate program, what can you do today to bring new affiliates on board where you pay them for bringing you new business?

What kind of loyalty program do/could you have in place to encourage customers to come back and buy more from you instead of shopping somewhere else?

What bounceback offers do you have to bring customers back for their next purchase?

What kinds of consumables does/could your business offer?

How can you repackage or reformulate your product to appeal to a different kind of buyer?

What updates can you make to your product or service to encourage customers to come back and buy the same thing they already have, but newer?

When was your last customer appreciation event? What kind of event could you organize to thank your customers, get introduced to their friends, and showcase your latest offerings?

All of these ideas will help to increase the Frequency and Amount of Transactions and the overall Customer Lifetime Value.

Expense Reduction

In looking at reducing your expenses, you're going to want a few reports handy.

First is your Profit and Loss reports (P&L).

Next up is your vendor report (a summary of how much you've paid each vendor).

These can easily be exported from your bookkeeping software, or by your bookkeeper.

When looking at your P&L, what are your top 3-5 spending categories?

When was the last time you reached out to those vendors to ask about lowering your bills? Which ones can you reach out to today to start the expense reduction conversation?

When looking at your list of vendors, do you still need all the services you're paying for?

When was the last time you reviewed your health insurance plan? Given your company's claim history, what can they do to lower your costs?

Review your telecom/wireless bills. Call your providers and ask for a better rate. Speak to their customer retention department if you need to.

Assess your office space. Are you paying too much rent for too large of a space? Can your landlord lower your rent?

Look at your software and SaaS expenses. Do you need all that you're paying for? What software can you get lifetime access to or discounts with an annual payment? Do you need the seats / plan that you're currently paying for?

Fast Action Plan

Now... given all of the ideas and strategies from the previous pages... What are your top five that you want to get done, right away, in order?

1.

2.

3.

4.

5.

When are you going to implement these? Pull out your calendar and block the time right now.

Good. Now go get 'em done!

15. Beyond the Book

"Knowing is half the battle!", as they say in G.I.Joe. But what's the other half?

Well, you even created your personalized Action Plan in the last chapter. So that's done. (Right?)

Implementation?

You know that already. And you've hopefully already started on making some of the changes from your Action Plan.

Going at it alone and finding all the things that don't work?

That's not super fun, or a great use of time.

What happens when you have questions? Or want a hand in filling out your action plan? Or need assistance in implementing?

We're here to help.

From 1:1 engagements to help you finalize your Action Plan, answer your questions, and get you started, to coaching you each step of the way, to helping out with actual implementation, we're here for you.

We are a community of like-minded entrepreneurs and have been helping business owners like you to get unstuck.

You don't need to go at this alone. There's no prize for learning everything the hard and slow way when there are others there to help you get there easier and faster.

Reach out, connect with us, and get the community and support you deserve.

Join us at YourBusinessGrowthPlaybook.com today.

To your success,

Jeremy Shapiro

"Jeremy's energy, geniality and enthusiasm are a marvelous complement to his depth of knowledge regarding startups and entrepreneurship!" – Hersh Rephun

"Jeremy Shapiro offers clear, actionable insights on scaling businesses and achieving entrepreneurial freedom. Highly recommended!" – Shihan Sheriff, MoneyMasterHQ

"Jeremy is helping entrepreneurs step out of struggle and into scale!" – Alex Sanfilippo, PodMatch

"The wisdom Jeremy shared helped me build smarter systems, focus on profit, not just revenue, and ultimately scale the business to the point where I was able to exit successfully." – Ryan Crownholm, MySitePlan and DirtMatch

"Jeremy is a highly skilled deeply thoughtful innovator and someone you want by your side in business." – Stephan Little, Zero Limits Capital

"I've seen firsthand Jeremy's exceptional coaching skills and deep knowledge, I wholeheartedly recommend him. His dedication to empowering entrepreneurs is truly inspiring." – Avik Chakraborty, Healthy Mind

Strategy Index by Niche

While this book encompasses a wealth of great strategies that can be used in *most* any business, certain strategies work best in certain niches/industries.

Find your niche below for a quick reference to our favorite strategies just for you! Remember, these aren't the *only* ones for you to use, just the best ones to get started with.

And if you're already using some of strategies listed for your niche, the referenced chapters may still be worth another read for inspiration or a reminder of how others are doing what you're doing slightly differently.

Best Strategies for Subscription / SaaS / Membership Businesses

If the core of your business is already built around recurring revenue, these specific strategies are your low hanging fruit to start with.

- **Subscriptions / Membership / Continuity**: This is the core of your business model, focusing on providing ongoing value to customers for recurring payments, leading to predictable revenue.

- **Customer Lifetime Value (CLV)**: Crucial for understanding the long-term worth of your customers, allowing you to make informed decisions about customer acquisition and retention, even when the initial sale might be low or at a loss.

- **Sloanism - Ongoing Updates**: For SaaS and software businesses, releasing updated models or versions annually encourages repeat purchases or continued subscriptions, even if the existing product is already established and working.

- **Additional Product / Service Tiers**: Offering different membership levels (e.g., Basic, Premium) allows customers to ascend or descend based on their needs, helping to retain them and increase the amount they spend over time.

- **Upsells / Add-Ons**: Can significantly increase the Amount of Each Transaction by offering higher-tier plans or additional features at the point of sale.

- **Fixing Your Broken Funnels**: Optimizing conversion rates from prospects to paying subscribers (e.g., from free trial to paid) by addressing leaky stages, improving continuity, and ensuring lead quality.

- **Affiliates / Partners**: Leveraging others' audiences can be a highly scalable way to acquire new subscribers, with platforms like ClickBank and Amazon Associates built on this model for recurring revenue products.

- **Prepaid Options for Recurring Sales**: Encourage customers to pay for longer periods upfront (e.g., annual subscriptions), which can significantly increase the initial transaction amount and CLV, often by offering a discount for prepaying.

- **Strategies for Reducing Churn**: Directly impacts the longevity of your customer relationships and Customer Lifetime Value (CLV). Understanding and addressing the four common cancellation reasons (No Money, No Time, No Value, Too Complicated) can save many cancellations.

Best Strategies for High Ticket Products / Services

Already selling a high ticket product or service, in the 4-6 figure range? Fantastic! These strategies will help you expand wider and deeper with what you're already doing.

- **Increasing your Prices**: Often the most direct way to increase the Amount of Each Transaction, especially when your business provides high value or lacks perceived competition. Overcome mental blocks by focusing on value-based pricing.

- **Be the Bank with Payment Plans**: Offering multi-pay options (e.g., two payments instead of one lump sum) can lower the barrier to entry for higher-priced offerings, increasing both the Amount and Quantity of sales.

- **Third Party Financing Partners**: Leverage financing companies to underwrite the purchase, allowing customers to pay over time while you receive (almost) full payment upfront. This is particularly effective for very high-end sales.

- **The Power of Niching**: Specializing in a niche – or even more niche - segment allows you to differentiate from generalists, command higher prices, and be perceived as the expert in that niche.

- **Customization / Personalization**: Customers are willing to pay a premium for products or services that are tailored or personalized to their specific needs, increasing the perceived value, and in turn price.

- **Upsells / Add-Ons**: Strategically offer additional, often high-margin, services or products at the point of initial purchase (e.g., expedite fees, installation services) to increase the overall transaction amount.

- **Bundling for Profit**: Combine multiple related products or services into a package to increase the perceived value and justify a higher price, often without significantly increasing your costs.

- **Cold Calling / Telemarketing**: For B2B or certain high-ticket consumer services, direct outbound calls can be effective for setting qualified appointments for sales calls, leading to high-value conversions.

- **Media / Press / PR**: Earned media coverage builds credibility and authority, enhancing your company's reputation and supporting premium pricing without direct advertising costs.

Best Strategies for Professional Services

Is your business built around working one-on-one with clients and your current method of scaling is adding more team members to handle more clients? There *is* a better way. These strategies will help you to expand beyond just your professional service model.

- **Additional Product / Service Tiers**: Transition from purely one-on-one services by offering tiered levels such as "I'll show you how to do it" (e.g., courses), "I do it with you" (e.g., group coaching), and "I do it for you" (e.g., bespoke consulting). This caters to different client needs and price points.

- **Expanding Your Product Portfolio**: Introduce new offerings that complement your core service. For example, a doctor added a wellness membership program, and an estate planning attorney added an annual continuity program, creating new revenue streams and increasing client engagement.

- **Increasing your Prices**: Implement value-based pricing rather than hourly rates. A client 10xed her price by focusing on the client's desired outcome rather than her time.

- **The Power of Niching**: Become a specialist in a specific industry or client type (e.g., a business valuation firm focusing on three key industries) to attract ideal clients more effectively and justify higher fees.

- **Payment Plans / Third Party Financing**: For higher-cost service packages, offering payment options makes your services more accessible, increasing the Amount of Each Transaction and converting more prospects.

- **Referrals**: Cultivate strong relationships with referral partners who serve the same ideal customer but offer complementary services (e.g., a real estate agent and a mortgage broker). This is often the primary source of warm leads for professional services.

- Content Marketing / **SEO**: Establish yourself as a thought leader and attract clients by creating valuable content that answers their questions and solves their problems, improving your visibility in search results.

- **Cold Outbound Emailing** / Cold Calling: For B2B professional services, direct outreach is often the most scalable way to generate qualified leads and set sales appointments.

- **Customer Appreciation Events**: Host exclusive events for past and existing clients. This not only shows appreciation but can also re-engage them, leading to new projects or updated services, as seen with a high end portrait photography business.

Best Strategies for Coaches / Consultants

Do you personally work directly with clients and find yourself plateauing because everything depends on your one-on-one client work? These strategies are the fastest path to move beyond that.

- **Additional Product / Service Tiers**: Implement the "I'll show you how to do it" (e.g., online courses), "I do it with you" (e.g., group coaching, mastermind groups), and "I do it for you" (e.g., high-end one-on-one consulting) model. This leverages your time and appeals to different client budgets.

- **Expanding Your Product Portfolio**: Beyond tiered services, consider adding entirely new products like a mobile app (like Wim Hof) or niche-specific content that can generate recurring revenue or attract a broader audience.

- **Increasing your Prices**: Embrace value-based pricing for your coaching and consulting, moving away from hourly rates. The example of the client who 10xed her price illustrates the power of this.

- **The Power of Niching**: By specializing, you become the go-to expert for a specific problem or audience, allowing you to command higher fees and attract more ideal clients.

- **Payment Plans / Third Party Financing**: Make your high-ticket coaching programs more accessible by offering installment plans or leveraging third-party financing, increasing conversion rates for premium offers.

- **Affiliates / Partners**: Collaborate with other experts or businesses who have an audience of your ideal clients. They promote your offerings in exchange for a commission, allowing you to reach new markets without direct marketing spend.

- **Content Marketing / SEO**: Create valuable content (e.g., blog posts, videos, podcasts) that positions you as an authority, answers common questions, and attracts organic traffic from potential clients searching for solutions.

- **Media / Press / PR**: Seek opportunities for earned media (interviews, features) to build your personal brand and credibility, which is vital for attracting high-end coaching and consulting clients.

- **Customer Appreciation Events**: Host exclusive events or webinars for your existing and past clients. These events foster community, deepen relationships, and can naturally lead to new engagements or referrals.

Best Strategies for E-Commerce Businesses

Is your core business selling products direct to consumers online from your website or third party marketplaces? These strategies will help you to do more!

- **Subscriptions / Membership / Continuity**: Implement "Subscribe and Save" programs (like Amazon's) or auto-ship options for consumable products, providing convenience to customers and predictable recurring revenue.

- **Expanding Your Product Portfolio**: Continuously launch new products that appeal to your existing customer base. An e-commerce client fast-tracked growth by dedicating a team to frequent new product releases, often selling out to existing customers before public launch.

- **Loyalty Programs**: Create a VIP program (like Zappos') that rewards frequent buyers with perks like free expedited shipping, easy returns, or exclusive access to new products. This builds strong customer loyalty and increases Frequency of Transactions.

- **Consumables**: If your product isn't naturally consumable, consider introducing related consumables that customers will repurchase regularly (e.g., coffee pods for a coffee maker).

- **Repacking / Reformulating**: Offer different quantities or formulations of your products (e.g., smaller packs at higher unit prices, multipacks at a discount) to cater to various customer needs and encourage more frequent or larger purchases.

- **Upsells / Add-Ons**: Integrate impulse buys or relevant add-ons during the online checkout process. Free shipping offers for exceeding a certain cart value can also significantly increase the Amount of Each Transaction.

- **Tiered Bonuses by Purchase Amount**: Offer free gifts, extended warranties, or other perks when customers reach specific spending thresholds. Studies show this can increase average order value significantly.

- **Volume Discounts for Quantity**: Encourage larger initial purchases by offering price breaks for buying multiple units of the same item. This leverages the fixed customer acquisition cost.

- **Pay Per Click (PPC) Advertising**: Platforms like Google Ads and Amazon's PPC are essential for driving targeted traffic to your product listings and scaling customer acquisition.

- **Search Engine Optimization (SEO)**: Optimize product pages and content to rank highly in search engine results, attracting organic traffic from customers actively looking for your products.

- **Social Media**: Build a community around your brand and use engaging content to drive traffic and sales, but remember to move followers onto your own list for direct communication.

- **Affiliates / Partners**: Leverage affiliate programs (like Amazon Associates) to have others promote your products to their audience in exchange for a commission, expanding your reach.

- **Bounceback Offers**: Include inserts in packages or offer follow-up emails with promotions or incentives to encourage repeat purchases directly from your store, bypassing marketplaces.

Best Strategies for Info-Product Businesses

Is your primary product information marketing, like books, courses, classes, workshops, and live events? These proven strategies work best for businesses just like yours.

- **Subscriptions / Membership / Continuity**: Offer membership sites, ongoing programs, or paid newsletters that provide continuous value (e.g., updated content, community access) beyond a one-time course purchase. The Wim Hof app is a great example.

- **Expanding Your Product Portfolio**: Develop complementary info-products or repurpose existing content for new formats or niches. Authors often re-niche their books (e.g., *Magnetic Marketing for Lawyers*) to appeal to specific audiences.

- **Additional Product / Service Tiers**: Create different tiers for your info-products (e.g., basic course, premium course with coaching, live event access). The Financial Times model of print-only, digital-only, and combined subscriptions applies here.

- **Bundling for Profit**: Combine multiple info-products or add bonuses from partner companies into attractive bundles. An info/education company successfully bundled recorded presentations, transcripts, and summaries to increase sales and profit.

- **Be the Bank with Payment Plans**: For higher-priced courses or programs, offering installment plans (e.g., a two-pay option) can make them more accessible and boost enrollment without discounting the overall price.

- **Third Party Financing Partners**: For very high-end courses or masterminds, use external financing partners to allow customers to pay over time, receiving your revenue upfront.

- **Affiliate Offers**: Info-product businesses often have high profit margins, allowing for generous affiliate commissions. Leveraging affiliates with relevant audiences can drive significant new customer acquisition.

- **Search Engine Optimization (SEO) / Content Marketing**: Create valuable, original content that answers prospects' questions and positions you as an expert. This helps your info-products appear in relevant searches and attracts organic traffic.

- **Pay Per Click (PPC) Advertising**: Drive targeted traffic to your landing pages for lead magnets, webinars, or direct sales of info-products. Effective PPC requires a congruent funnel and active management.

- **Social Media**: Build a community around your expertise, share insights, and use Calls to Action (CTAs) to direct engaged followers to your lead magnets or offers. Consider private groups for deeper engagement.

- **Media / Press / PR**: Leverage your expertise to get featured in relevant publications, podcasts, or media outlets. This builds credibility and expands your reach to new audiences.

- **Downsells**: If a prospect declines a high-priced info-product, offer a lower-cost alternative (e.g., a mini-course, a single module, or a book) to convert them into a paying customer at a lower entry point.

- **Consumables**: Even information products can have a consumable element, like the *Five Minute Journal* which encourages repeat purchases due to its structure and use.

Best Strategies for Retail Stores

Do you have a physical retail store where most of your business comes from customers walking into your store and making a purchase in person? These strategies work best in your niche.

- **Bounceback Offers**: Provide incentives at the point of sale (e.g., printed on receipts, or a small card) to encourage customers to return for a second purchase within a limited time. This is commonly seen in restaurants but applies to retail.

- **Loyalty Programs**: Implement punch cards, tiered rewards systems, or mobile apps (like Starbucks') that incentivize repeat visits and purchases. Customers with "sunk costs" in points are less likely to shop elsewhere.

- **Customer Appreciation Events**: Host exclusive in-store events for past and existing customers. This can re-engage them, showcase new offerings, and encourage immediate purchases, as demonstrated by a client opening a new retail location.

- **Consumables**: If applicable, highlight or introduce consumable products that require frequent repurchase (e.g., coffee pods for a machine you sell, bicycle tire tubes for the bikes you sell, or stationery that gets used).

- **Repacking / Reformulating**: Offer products in different quantities or package sizes. The example of zip-top bags at Target vs. Costco shows how varying quantities can encourage both more frequent visits or larger bulk buys.

- **Upsells / Add-Ons**: Strategically place impulse buy items near checkout counters. Train staff to offer relevant add-ons or upgrades (e.g., an extended warranty on an appliance, or an accessory with a clothing purchase) to increase the Amount of Each Transaction.

- **Volume Discounts for Quantity**: Offer price breaks for buying multiple units of the same item (e.g., "buy 2, get 1 free," or a lower unit price for larger packs) to encourage customers to spend more upfront.

- **Tiered Bonuses by Purchase Amount**: Provide a free gift or bonus when a customer's purchase exceeds a certain amount, encouraging them to add more to their cart.

- **Local SEO**: Essential for ensuring your physical store appears prominently in local search results and Google Maps listings (Google My Business, Apple Business Connect). Maintain consistent NAP information across directories.

- **Direct Mail**: Use targeted direct mail campaigns to attract new customers within your geographic service area, as successfully done by a brick-and-mortar retail store client.

- **Traditional Advertising**: Utilize local newspapers, radio, or community magazines to build brand awareness and attract foot traffic from your target audience.

- **Referrals**: Encourage word-of-mouth referrals from satisfied customers and build relationships with local businesses that serve your ideal customer (e.g., a sports store hosting a race bib pickup)

Best Strategies for B2B Businesses

Do you sell to businesses? These strategies work best for B2B businesses.

- **Subscriptions / SaaS / Membership**: Many B2B businesses operate on recurring revenue models (e.g., SaaS). This ensures predictable cash flow and ongoing customer relationships.

- **The Power of Niching**: Specialize in serving a particular industry or type of business to establish yourself as the go-to vendor. A business valuation firm found success by dialing in their positioning for specific industries, commanding higher prices.

- **Cold Outbound Emailing**: A highly effective and scalable strategy for B2B lead generation. Create targeted lists of decision-makers and send email campaigns to get them to "raise their hand" for a discovery or sales call.

- **Cold Calling / Telemarketing**: Implement a structured outbound calling strategy to qualify suspects and set appointments for sales representatives, a highly scalable method for B2B client acquisition.

- **Affiliates / Partners**: Develop strong relationships with complementary B2B businesses that share your ideal customer. They can refer qualified leads to you, as seen with a SaaS business partnering with others in the same market.

- **Expanding Your Product Portfolio**: Identify additional products or services that your business clients need, even if outside your core offering. A locksmithing business successfully cross-sold camera and security systems to its access control clients.

- **Additional Product / Service Tiers**: Offer tiered service levels (e.g., "I'll show you," "I do it with you," "I do it for you") to cater to businesses of different sizes or with varying needs and budgets.

- **Payment Plans / Third Party Financing Partners**: For high-value B2B contracts, offering flexible payment options (installments or third-party financing) can close more deals by reducing the upfront financial commitment for your clients.

- **Search Engine Optimization (SEO) / Content Marketing**: Create valuable content that addresses the specific challenges and questions of your B2B audience. This attracts organic traffic, establishes thought leadership, and feeds your sales funnel.

- **Pay Per Click (PPC) Advertising**: Target businesses with specific problems or needs using platforms like Google Ads. Effective PPC, with a congruent funnel, can deliver high-quality leads.

- **Social Media**: Utilize platforms like LinkedIn for B2B networking, content sharing, and building private communities where qualified prospects can engage with your brand.

- **Media / Press / PR**: Earned media coverage in industry publications or business news outlets builds immense credibility and visibility within your target market, positioning you as a trusted expert.

- **Expand Up Your Supply Chain**: Analyze your biggest expenses. If you're spending a lot with a particular vendor, consider bringing that function in-house or acquiring a supplier, as Zingerman's did with their bread, dairy, and coffee.

Glossary

Additive: Something is additive when you add/sum the numbers together. See also Multiplicative.

Affiliate Partner: An affiliate is a person or company that promotes your products or services in exchange for a commission.

Affiliate Program: An affiliate program is a partnership where you pay individuals or companies (affiliates or referral partners) a commission for referring new leads or customers to your business.

Amount of Each Transaction: This refers to how much a customer spends each time they make a purchase from your business. Increasing this amount is one of the three major levers you can pull to grow your revenue and profit.

Apple Business Connect (ABC): ABC is Apple's equivalent of Google My Business (GMB) for Apple Maps. It allows you to create and manage your business's presence on Apple Maps, which is important for Local SEO (Search Engine Optimization), especially for customers using Siri or other Apple products.

Blue Ocean: This refers to a market without existing competition, where new demand is created. Businesses in a Blue Ocean can differentiate themselves and command higher prices because there are no perceived alternatives by prospective customers. Contrast that with a Red Ocean where competition is high, products are commoditized, and companies compete on price.

Bounceback Offer: A bounceback offer is a marketing strategy used to encourage customers to make a repeat purchase after they have already transacted with you. Typically, this offer is given to the customer after their initial purchase and is valid for a limited time. Bounceback offers often take the form of a discount, a free item (like a free appetizer), or a buy-one-get-one (BOGO) deal.

Business to Business (B2B): B2B refers to transactions or business conducted between two companies, rather than between a company and individual consumers.

Call to Action (CTA): A clear, inviting prompt that encourages an audience to take a specific, desired action, often used in marketing materials to guide prospects on what to do next. For example a CTA might be inviting a reader to opt-in, schedule a call, or make a purchase.

Churn: Churn is the percentage of recurring revenue customers you lose in a specific time period compared to the number of customers you had at the beginning of that period. Understanding and reducing churn is important for maximizing Customer Lifetime Value (CLV).

Click Through Rate (CTR): This is a metric used in online marketing, particularly in relation to ads. It represents the percentage of people who see your ad (impression) and then click on it.

Consumable: These are products that customers need to repurchase regularly as they use them up. Businesses built on a consumable model, like those selling razor blades or coffee pods, benefit from a high Frequency of Transactions.

Cost of Goods Sold (COGS): This represents the direct costs associated with producing the goods or services that your business sells. Gross Sales minus COGS (and other factors) contributes to your Gross Profit. COGS are different than expenses which are the broader costs related to running the business. COGS relate directly to your sales volume as they are part of every sale.

Cost Per Acquisition (CPA): This is a performance metric in advertising that tells you how much it costs you, on average, to acquire a new paying customer through a specific marketing campaign. It's calculated by dividing your total ad spend by the number of customers acquired from that campaign.

Cost Per Action (CPA): CPA, like PPC, is a form of online advertising, but you pay per Action a person takes, like filling out a form, downloading an app, or making a purchase.

Cost Per Click (CPC): This is a metric used in Pay Per Click (PPC) advertising and represents the amount you pay each time someone clicks on your online advertisement. See also CTR.

Cross sell: A cross sell is when you offer a customer a complementary product or service that is related to what they are already purchasing. Unlike upsells, which are typically upgrades or additions to the primary purchase, cross-sells cater to the same audience but are not directly tied to the initial item.

Customer: A customer is an individual or business that purchases your products or services. The goal of your business is to not just acquire customers but to create lifetime customers.

Customer Acquisition Cost (CAC): This is the total cost your business incurs to acquire a new customer. Understanding your CAC is crucial for evaluating the efficiency of your marketing and sales efforts. Having a strong profit margin up front allows you to invest more in acquiring customers.

Customer Lifetime Value (CLV): This represents the total revenue a single customer is expected to generate for your business over the entire duration of your relationship with them. Understanding and increasing your CLV allows you to outspend your competition on acquiring new customers and focus on long-term profitability.

Customer Relationship Management (CRM): A CRM is a system or tool used to manage and organize your interactions with current and potential customers. These systems can help you track each step in your sales funnels and provide data on your sales numbers, stats, and other metrics.

Decacorn: A decacorn is a business with a value over $10 billion dollars. The word is a combination of *Deca*, for the unit of ten, and *Unicorn* meaning a business valued at over $1 billion dollars.

Downsell: A downsell is a lower-priced offer that you present to a potential customer when they decide not to purchase your main, higher-priced product or service. The aim of a downsell is to still capture some revenue from a prospect and convert them into a customer, even at a lower price point.

Frequency of Transactions: This refers to how often your customers make purchases from your business. Increasing this frequency is one of the three key levers for scaling your revenue and profits.

Funnel: A funnel describes the journey a potential customer takes from first becoming aware of your business to eventually making a purchase. At each stage of the funnel, some potential customers will drop off, hence the "funnel" shape. Understanding and optimizing each step of your funnel helps you increase the Quantity of Customers coming out of the bottom of your funnel.

Google My Business (GMB): Now known as Google Business Profile, GMB is a free tool from Google that allows you to manage your business's online presence across Google, including Search and Maps. Optimizing your GMB profile is an important part of Local SEO.

Gross Sales: Also known as Gross Revenue, this is the total amount of money your business earns from all its sales during a specific period, before any deductions like costs, expenses, or refunds.

Hyper Buyers: Hyper buyers are customers who tend to purchase disproportionately more than a typical customer and they will often buy most anything you offer. The Frequency of their Transactions is much higher than average.

Impressions: Impressions refer to the number of times your content, such as an ad, is displayed to users. This is a metric typically tracked at the Top of Your Funnel (ToFu) and is particularly relevant in Pay Per Click (PPC) advertising. While in PPC you generally pay for clicks, generating a sufficient number of impressions among your target audience increases your visibility and the potential for engagement.

Key Performance Indicator (KPI): KPIs are measurable values that demonstrate how effectively a company is achieving key business objectives. Examples of metrics discussed that could serve as KPIs include Click Through Rate (CTR), Cost Per Click (CPC), Cost Per Acquisition (CPA), conversion rates at each stage of your funnel, Customer Lifetime Value (CLV), and churn. Regularly monitoring these indicators helps you understand what's working and identify areas for improvement.

Lead: A lead is a potential customer who has shown interest in your products or services. This interest is often demonstrated by taking an action such as opting into your email list, scheduling a call, or filling out an application.

Lead Magnet: A lead magnet is a valuable piece of content or an offer that you provide to potential customers in exchange for their contact information, typically their email address. The purpose of a lead magnet is to attract qualified prospects and build your list, thereby moving them further down your marketing funnel. Examples of lead magnets could include free guides, checklists, templates, or the first chapter of a book.

Mastermind Group: A Mastermind Group is a gathering of like-minded individuals who meet regularly to share their experiences, offer support, and hold each other accountable for achieving their goals. These groups provide a space for members to exchange ideas, get feedback, and avoid feeling like they have to navigate business challenges alone.

Minimum Viable Product (MVP): An MVP is the simplest version of a new product that allows a team to learn the most about customers and validate their ideas with the least effort. The idea is to launch an MVP first to test market interest and traction before expanding the product or funnel.

Multiplicative: This refers to when numbers are multiplied together (as opposed to added). F x A x Q, for example, is multiplicative. This means that even a small percentage increase in each of the three levers can result in a significantly larger overall increase in your gross sales than if those same percentage increases were simply added together.

NAP (Name, Address, Phone Number): NAP refers to the consistent listing of your business name, physical address, and phone number across various online directories and platforms, which is crucial for local SEO and establishing relevance in local search results.

Niche: A niche refers to a specialized segment of a larger market. By specializing in a certain niche, a business can become more valuable and command a higher price. Within a broader niche, many subgroups exist, and creating offers to serve these niches can expand your product portfolio and attract new customers.

Opt-In: An opt-in is an action by a potential customer to show interest in your products or services, typically by providing their contact information, such as an email address, in exchange for a lead magnet or to receive updates. A low opt-in rate in a funnel can indicate a lack of continuity between your ad copy and the landing page or targeting and the offer.

Pay Per Click (PPC): PPC is a model where you only pay when someone clicks on your ad, rather than for the ad being displayed (impressions). Examples of PPC platforms include Google AdWords, Facebook Ads, and Amazon's PPC platform. While PPC can deliver great results, it requires a congruent funnel and active management. Poor targeting in PPC can lead to low-quality leads in your funnel.

Plateau: A plateau in a business occurs when growth stagnates and the strategies that previously led to success are no longer working, leaving you feeling stuck.

Profit: Profit is the financial gain remaining after deducting expenses from income (revenue).

Profit and Loss Statement (P&L): A P&L is a financial report that summarizes a company's revenues, costs, and expenses over a specific period, showing the net profit or loss. This report is available in your bookkeeping software or can be prepared for you by your bookkeeper.

Prospect: A prospect is someone who is potentially interested in your products or services but has not yet made a purchase. Your marketing aims to attract prospects and guide them through your funnel to become customers. Prospects - unlike suspects - have shown interest in your business.

Public Relations (PR): PR involves efforts to manage and shape public perception of your business through earned media, such as news articles and features in publications, rather than paid advertising.

Quantity of Customers: This refers to the total number of unique customers who buy from your business. Increasing the quantity of customers is the third of your three major levers for scaling revenue.

Red Ocean: A market characterized by intense competition where businesses fight over existing demand, often leading to commoditization and companies competing on price. Contrast that with a blue ocean where there is no competition, demand is created, and businesses can charge what they like.

Referral Partner: A referral partner is an individual or business with a network or audience of your ideal customers who is willing to recommend your products or services to them. Referral partners differ from affiliates in that referrals are typically more personal and warm and don't usually involve a direct financial reward at the time of the referral.

Repositioning: Repositioning involves presenting your existing products or services to new customer profiles or markets by tailoring your messaging and approach to their specific needs. This strategy allows you to find new avenues for growth with your current offerings.

Return on Ad Spend (RoAS): RoAS is a metric used to measure the effectiveness of your advertising campaigns. It represents the revenue generated for every dollar spent on advertising. To calculate, divide the gross revenue generated from your ad by the cost of the ad. Higher is better.

Return on Investment (ROI): Broader than RoAS, ROI is a more general financial metric that measures the profitability of an investment. It compares the gain or loss from an investment relative to its cost. To calculate, divide how much you made from something by how much was invested. A positive ROI indicates that the investment is profitable.

Sales Development Rep (SDR): An SDR is a person whose job it is to contact cold *suspects* and turn them into qualified *prospects* at which point they get handed over to a sales rep. Their job isn't to close any sales, rather to book meetings for the sales team.

Search Engine Optimization (SEO): SEO is the practice of optimizing your website and online content to improve its visibility in search engine results pages (SERPs). The goal of SEO is to attract organic (non-paid) traffic from users who are searching for information relevant to your business.

Search Engine Results Page (SERP): SERP is the page displayed by a search engine (like Google, Bing, etc.) in response to a user's search query. The goal of Search Engine Optimization (SEO) is to improve your website's ranking and visibility on the SERPs for relevant keywords, in turn attracting more organic traffic.

Software as a Service (SaaS): SaaS is a software distribution model where a third-party provider hosts applications and makes them available to customers online, often on a subscription basis. This is in contrast to the older more traditional model of selling software licenses.

Suspect: A suspect is an individual who fits your target audience profile but has had no prior interaction with your business. The initial goal when marketing to suspects is to generate interest and convert them into prospects.

Top of Your Funnel (ToFu): This is the initial stage of your marketing funnel where you aim to attract and capture the attention of a large audience of potential customers. Activities at this stage include things like impressions, clicks on ads, website visits, and opting into your email list. The goal is to fill the ToFu with qualified prospects.

Tripwire: A tripwire is a low-priced introductory offer designed to convert prospects into paying customers. The goal of a tripwire is to lower the barrier to entry for potential customers and allow them to experience the value of your offerings at a minimal cost. Once they have made this initial purchase, they are more likely to invest in your core products or services and move through your sales funnel.

Upsell: An upsell is where you encourage a customer to purchase a more expensive, upgraded, or premium version of the product or service they are already considering. Offering upsells at the time of purchase is a key strategy for increasing the Amount of Each Transaction.

Impact at Scale

One of the most powerful parts about entrepreneurship is how it can change lives. Not just the life of the business owner, but their family, and their community at large.

Entrepreneurship provides more than just revenue, financial freedom, and entrepreneurial freedom; it provides jobs and value to the market.

Entrepreneurship can literally change the world.

Case in point, since 1987, Village Enterprise has trained over 300,000 entrepreneurs in sub-Saharan Africa. These entrepreneurs have teamed up to start over 100,000 businesses, transforming over 2,000,000 lives.

All through entrepreneurship.

In addition, of over 225,000 nonprofits evaluated worldwide by Charity Navigator, Village Enterprise is also one of only three nonprofits in the world to receive a perfect four-star 100% rating and the only international nonprofit with a perfect score.

Their training has elevated *millions* out of extreme poverty and the ripple effect is powerful.

One of my favorite stories from Village Enterprise is from one of their earlier students, and fellow serial entrepreneur, Hellen.

Hellen, a resident of Soroti, one of Uganda's most impoverished regions, had children to feed and educate. Business is still pretty much a man's world in Uganda and it can be difficult for women to get credit, but Hellen was able to secure a $300 business grant and training from Village Enterprise.

This small start enabled her to escape generational poverty, one entrepreneurial step at a time.

First, Hellen trained to become a tailor and used her start-up grant to rent a sewing machine and buy fabric, which allowed her to grow her tailoring business.

But Hellen was community-minded and didn't stop there. So, she purchased sewing machines, hired a part-time employee, and created a vocational school to train 40 other at-risk women to sew.

During school, however, Hellen saw her students arriving hungry, so she started a restaurant to feed them, and that restaurant now employs even more people! That in turn, became a catering business, serving food beyond just the school, like at weddings.

Hellen has also gone on to build a church and plans to create a hair salon and another school.

In Hellen's words: "I am so proud of myself - to think I came from so little and now have so much. And even still, it is going to grow!"

Hellen has not just escaped generational poverty, she has literally changed her entire community.

This is the power of entrepreneurship.

This is why we've partnered with Village Enterprise for so many years, sponsoring budding entrepreneurs like Hellen into their program.

As a proud member of 1% for the Planet, we've contributed over 1% of gross revenue (not profit, but gross sales) to select causes like Village Enterprise.

In fact, your purchase of this book directly helps to support causes like Village Enterprise.

If you'd like to see how you can help and support them even further, you can join me in supporting entrepreneurs like Hellen at: YourBusinessGrowthPlaybook.com/impact/

Acknowledgements

I remember the day I sat down and put pen to paper to start writing this book and thinking I'd have it done, wrapped and shipped in a few weeks. The writing came easy.

What I didn't know at the time was just how much goes into publishing a book intentionally that has nothing to do with actually writing.

Getting early feedback on the scope, reader profile, promise, intro, table of contents, then the actual content, the title, subtitle, covers, and so much more takes time. Not just to ask for the feedback, but to listen, to implement, and to repeat. I've learned so much during this process and couldn't have done it without some very special people I deeply appreciate.

I offer my deepest appreciation to:

The folks who provided feedback on my book's scope, reader profile, intro, title, covers, and the entire manuscript: George Sudarkoff, Peter Mu, Amira Richler, Ben Towne, Stephen Goldberg, Brian Bersbach, Dave Gilman, Amadeus Ciok, Dave McGrath, David Friedlander, Linda Balliro, Megan Preston Meyer, Emily Randall, Jenny Yu, Dom Cassone, Sherri Goodman, Nathan Amaral, Tom Fleming, Vandita Joshi, Pat Burns, Todd Flesner, Marc Freedman, Sara Lobkovich, Angelina Carleton, Max Johnson, Phil Masiello, Angela Frank, Megan Fluke, Junaid Ahmed, Shelley Timmins, Kara Schlindwein, Jody Shapiro, Matthew Dowling, Jason Troyer, L. Michael Burt, Michele Rosenthal, Antwon Lincoln, Gary Anderson, Brian Hall, Layne Gneiting, Shihan Sheriff, Jake Nguyen.

My fantastic wife, Emily Randall, for her endless support, encouragement, love, careful editing, tough questions, insightful perspectives, and adventurous spirit that's led us to so many great places around the world together and as a family.

Sheila Farragher-Gemma for asking how she could help me without looking for anything in return, showing me how Givers Gain, and teaching me the importance of the real priorities in life.

David Hilton for coaching and mentorship, asking great questions, and knowing how to get me to do things that are good for me even though I might not realize it until after.

Tom Fleming for his friendship and mentorship, putting me on a stage for the first time, showing me how to dial for dollars, and helping me to pick "what's next" in a world of opportunity.

Yanik Silver for being the light that inspired a thousand suns and connecting me with so many wonderful humans, experiences, adventures, and ideas.

My wonderful clients and mastermind members who believe in me, look to me for guidance, take the leaps of faith in testing our ideas in their business, get out of their comfort zone for their own good, and share their time and results.

Albert Griesmayr for his brilliant keyword research and help with categories, publishing, and titling.

Hugh Barker for his careful editing, thoughtful developmental feedback, attention to detail, and appreciation for grammar, clarity, and curly quotes.

Robbie Samuels for encouraging me to ask for pre-publication reviews and leading by example.

Julie Broad and Rob Fitzpatrick for each creating wonderful communities of fellow non-fiction authors to connect, learn, and grow.

Caerus Kourt for their intentional cover design research, process, creativity, and refinement. And for putting up with my analytical approach to quantitative feedback.

About the Author

Jeremy B. Shapiro is a serial-entrepreneur. Since 1996, every single one of his many businesses have been in the service of fellow entrepreneurs.

For decades, through structured mastermind groups, workshops, one-on-one coaching, and consulting work, Jeremy has been helping entrepreneurs discover the core strengths in themselves and their business, and realize their true potential combining passion and expertise to grow their businesses and attain the freedom they deserve.

In his role as a mentor and coach to entrepreneurs, Jeremy has helped small business owners make the transition from "solopreneur" to "business owner" – an important distinction that many entrepreneurs can easily miss when working "in" their business instead of "on" their business.

Jeremy has been interviewed extensively by the media for his expert opinions and has been interviewed and featured on NPR Morning Edition, the Boston Business Journal, Fox News, ABC, NBC, PBS, the Boston Globe, New England Cable News, The Australian, California Biz Journal, Market Watch, and Toyo Keizai – the Business Week of Japan.

When not helping other entrepreneurs take their businesses to the next level, you'll likely find Jeremy traveling the world with his family, soaking up language and culture like a sponge, cycling unreasonably long distances for vegan pastries and craft coffee, running, or cooking for friends and family.

Visit YourBusinessGrowthPlaybook.com to connect with Jeremy.

www.ingramcontent.com/pod-product-compliance
Lightning Source LLC
Chambersburg PA
CBHW071543210326
41597CB00019B/3097